The Inner Life

Inner Land

A Guide into the Heart of the Gospel

■ □ □ □ □ **The Inner Life**
The Inner Life
The Heart
Soul and Spirit

□ ■ □ □ □ **The Conscience**
The Conscience and Its Witness
The Conscience and Its Restoration

□ □ ■ □ □ **Experiencing God**
The Experience of God
The Peace of God

□ □ □ ■ □ **Fire and Spirit**
Light and Fire
The Holy Spirit

□ □ □ □ ■ **The Living Word**

Volume 1

The Inner Life

Eberhard Arnold

PLOUGH PUBLISHING HOUSE

Published by Plough Publishing House
Walden, New York, USA
Robertsbridge, East Sussex, UK
Elsmore, NSW, Australia

Plough is the publishing house of the Bruderhof, an international community of families and singles seeking to follow Jesus together. Members of the Bruderhof are committed to a way of radical discipleship in the spirit of the Sermon on the Mount. Inspired by the first church in Jerusalem (Acts 2 and 4), they renounce private property and share everything in common in a life of nonviolence, justice, and service to neighbors near and far. To learn more about the Bruderhof's faith, history, and daily life, see Bruderhof.com.

ISBN 978-0-87486-167-9

22 21 20 19   1 2 3 4 5 6

Translated from the 1936 edition of *Innen Land: Ein Wegweiser in die Seele der Bibel und in den Kampf um die Wirklichkeit* (Buchverlag des Almbruderhof e. V.) This edition is based on the 1975 English edition translated by Winifred Hildel and Miriam Potts.

Cover image: *Big Sky* (oil on canvas) by Erin Hanson, copyright © Erin Hanson. Used with permission.

A catalog record for this book is available from the British Library.
Library of Congress Cataloging-in-Publication Data

Names: Arnold, Eberhard, 1883-1935, author.
Title: The inner life / Eberhard Arnold.
Other titles: Innenland. English
Description: Walden NY : Plough Publishing House, 2019. | Series: Inner land:
   a guide into the heart of the Gospel ; Volume 1 | Previously published:
   c1999.
Identifiers: LCCN 2019016244 (print) | LCCN 2019019027 (ebook) | ISBN
   9780874861792 (pdf) | ISBN 9780874861679 (hardback)
Subjects: LCSH: Spiritual life--Bruderhof Communities. | Bruderhof
   Communities--Doctrines.
Classification: LCC BX8129.B65 (ebook) | LCC BX8129.B65 A72413
2019 (print) |
   DDC 248.4/897--dc23
LC record available at https://lccn.loc.gov/2019016244
Printed in the United States

Dedicated to my faithful wife,
Emmy Arnold

Contents

For this is the covenant that I will make with the house of Israel after those days, declares the Lord: I will put my law within them, and I will write it on their hearts. And I will be their God, and they shall be my people.

Jeremiah 31:33

Preface

Born to an academic family in the Prussian city of
Königsberg, Eberhard Arnold (1883–1935) received a
doctorate in philosophy and became a sought-after
writer and speaker in Germany. Yet like thousands
of other young Europeans in the turbulent years
following World War I, he and his wife, Emmy,
were disillusioned by the failure of the establishment – especially the churches – to provide answers
to the problems facing society.

In 1920, out of a desire to put into practice the
teachings of Jesus, the Arnolds turned their backs
on the privileges of middle-class life in Berlin and
moved to the village of Sannerz with their five young
children. There, with a handful of others, they started
an intentional community on the basis of the Sermon
on the Mount, drawing inspiration from the early
Christians and the sixteenth-century Anabaptists.
The community, which supported itself by agricul-
ture and publishing, attracted thousands of visitors
and eventually grew into the international movement
known as the Bruderhof.

Eberhard Arnold's magnum opus, *Inner Land* absorbed his energies off and on for most of his adult life. Begun in the months before World War I broke out, the first version of the book was published in 1914 as a patriotic pamphlet for German soldiers titled *War: A Call to Inwardness.* The first version to carry the title *Inner Land* appeared after the war in 1918; Arnold had extensively revised the text in light of his embrace of Christian pacifism. In 1932 Arnold began a new edit, reflecting the influence of religious socialism and his immersion in the writings of the sixteenth-century Radical Reformation, as well as his experiences living in the Sannerz community. Arnold continued to rework the book during the following three years, as he and the community became targets of increasing harassment as opponents of Nazism. The final text, on which this translation is based, was published in 1936. Arnold had died one year earlier as the result of a failed surgery.

This final version of *Inner Land* was not explicitly critical of the Nazi regime. Instead, it attacked the spirits that fed German society's support for Nazism: racism and bigotry, nationalistic fervor, hatred of political enemies, a desire for vengeance, and greed. At the same time, Arnold was not afraid to critique the evils of Bolshevism.

The chapter "Light and Fire," in particular, was a deliberate public statement at a decisive moment of Germany's history. Eberhard Arnold sent Hitler a copy on November 9, 1933. A week later the Gestapo raided the community and ransacked the author's study. After the raid, Eberhard Arnold had two Bruderhof members pack the already printed signatures

of *Inner Land* in watertight metal boxes and bury
them at night on the hill behind the community
for safekeeping. They later dug up *Inner Land* and
smuggled it out of the country, publishing it in Lich-
tenstein after Eberhard Arnold's death. Emmy Arnold
later fulfilled her husband's wish and added marginal
Bible references. (Footnotes are added by the editors.)

At first glance, the focus of *Inner Land* seems to
be the cultivation of the spiritual life. This would be
misleading. Eberhard Arnold writes:

> These are times of distress; they do not allow us
> to retreat just because we are willfully blind to the
> overwhelming urgency of the tasks that press upon
> human society. We cannot look for inner detachment
> in an inner and outer isolation. . . . The only thing
> that could justify withdrawing into the inner self
> to escape today's confusing, hectic whirl would be
> that fruitfulness is enriched by it. It is a question
> of gaining within, through unity with the eternal
> powers, that strength of character which is ready to
> be tested in the stream of the world.

Inner Land, then, calls us not to passivity, but to
action. It invites us to discover the abundance of a
life lived for God. It opens our eyes to the possibilities
of that "inner land of the invisible" where "our spirit
can find the roots of its strength." Only there, says
Eberhard Arnold, will we find the clarity of vision we
need to win the daily battle that is life, and the inner
anchor without which we will lose our moorings amid
the mass emotions and follies of the modern age.

The Editors

Introduction

The object of the book *Inner Land: A Guide into the Heart of the Gospel* [of which this volume contains only the introduction and the first three chapters] is to make an appeal in all the political, social, and economic upheaval today. It is an appeal for decision in the area of faith and beliefs, directed to the hearts of all those who do not want to forget or lose God and his ultimate kingdom. Using the events of contemporary history, this book attempts to point out that God's approaching judgment is aimed at our hearts, that the living Christ wants to move our innermost being through his quickening Spirit. Through this Spirit, who moves and stimulates everything, we are meant to gain, from within, a life that outwardly demonstrates justice, peace, and joy in the Holy Spirit, as a form of life shaped by God's active love.

Heb. 10:23–39

Rom. 14:17

In contrast to the path generally trodden today – one that tries to reach the inner life from the outside – this way must shine outward from within. Our spirit, received by the first man as God's breath, must first of all be at home in our innermost being;

Rom. 8:2

Gen. 2:7

our spirit must find the living roots of its strength there before it can press on to the periphery of life. Yet its calling is just this: to gain that mastery over

Gen. 1:26

all external things which to a large extent it has lost in the world of today. Man has lost his rulership over the earth and the just use of its wealth and resources because, through deep inner revolt, his spirit has been

Gen. 3:17–19

estranged from the breath of God and from his love.

This book, then, should bear witness to the way into the inner land of the invisible; it should bear witness to the way to God and to the Spirit and to love renewed again and again as the innermost experience of faith; and starting from here (for only then is it possible) it should bear witness to the best way to be effective as Christians.

Already before the [First] World War, several voices challenged Germans not to forget their mission to lead to the inner land of the invisible, to God and the Spirit. Out of an inner urge for fulfillment, they should point the way to new love, a way which is in accordance with humankind's calling. This urgent call, from Friedrich Lienhard and others, expressed the views of wide circles in Christian revivalism and in the German Youth Movement. Yet this call did not strike home. Therefore today (1932) at the eleventh hour it must find a voice more urgently than ever before. In the nationalistic fervor to exalt Germany's calling again, as it was more than a century ago, it must not be forgotten that the highest and the ultimate calling, even of Germans, is to become true men and women. This book is meant to help us consider that calling.

In this we may go along with Fichte (and all movements that are national in a true way) when he says:

> Blessed for me the hour when I decided to think about myself and my destiny. All my questions are answered; I know what it is possible for me to know; and I have no worries about what I cannot know. I am satisfied; there is perfect agreement and clarity in my spirit, for which a glorious new existence begins. What the whole of my destiny will be, I do not know: what I am to be and will become is beyond my comprehension. Part of this destiny is hidden from me, visible to One alone, the Father of Spirits, to whom it is entrusted. I only know that it is secure, and that it is eternal and glorious, as he himself is. But that part which is entrusted to me myself, I know thoroughly, and it is the root of all the rest of my knowledge.[1]

In recognizing this destiny, which the Father of Spirits alone sees quite clear and open before him, Fichte came progressively closer to the Bible. For him it was the book of those witnesses who were filled with the spirit of all good spirits, the book in which God's Spirit has found the deepest and purest expression. *Inner Land* is meant as a guide into the heart and soul of the Bible. The heart of the Bible is more than the letter. Even with the Bible, literal interpretation leads to spiritual death, to innermost untruthfulness. Only the Spirit who fills the heart of the Bible can lead us to its heart in spiritual freedom. Then the Spirit can lead us through that to the holy bond of a divine calling. The path this calling is to take starts in the human soul. Yet not for a moment

Rom. 7:6

John 5:39–40

2 Cor. 3:2–6

---

1 Johann Gottlieb Fichte, 1762–1814, *Die Bestimmung des Menschen.*

must this calling draw the soul away from God's history in the whole of humankind, away from God's calling in the world outside. *What is said in the Bible about the stirring of life in the soul, about the workings of the soul, and about its goal is to be interpreted and clearly presented in a concentrated form here.* With this, the book's task and its limitations could be considered well enough described. And yet *Inner Land* is not meant to serve some purely abstract purpose. Rather, as with the prophets and apostles of the Bible, its real task is to take hold of life vigorously and master it. Its aim is not theoretical discussion but something much more important: witnessing to an inner energy, an inner urge for practical expression, for work that is vital and has visible results.

At this point we cannot speak simply about the outward effects of this work: about the community life that arises out of it and the public responsibility involved. First of all, we have to speak about what is individual and personal – precisely this land of our inner being. Then it will become clear that a soul filled with the spirit of love cannot get stuck in individualism (which is the starting point), let alone in the private sphere of subjectivism. This soul, impressed by events in God's history, will gain power in its innermost depths from the Holy Spirit to intervene in history, making God's kingdom a reality.

For this, however, the deepest feeling, thought, and will of the soul must be enlightened and clarified. The conviction basic to this book is this proverb: "As a man thinks in his heart, so he is." Our attention should not be arrested by the dreary mixture of those outward habits, relationships, and subserviencies

Prov. 23:7

with which the life of an unfree soul exhausts itself. What is not clarified cannot lead us to God's kingdom either in inward or outward events. Only the pure Spirit of God can do this through the true human nature to which our innermost destiny calls us, hidden or buried though this true nature often is. It is with this final nature, the nature of the spirit created by God, that we must encounter God's Spirit, who calls us to his kingdom.

> My earthly deeds flow away in the stream of time, perceptions and feelings change, and not one can I hold on to. The scene I set up so easily for myself vanishes, and the stream always bears me on its steady wave toward new things. As often as I turn my gaze back into my inner self, though, I am immediately in the kingdom of eternity; I look upon the work of the Spirit, which no world can change and no time destroy, which itself creates world and time first of all.[2]

I do not share the point of view implied in these words of Schleiermacher, that the depths of God and the depths of the soul are one and the same depth; or that humans are part, breath, and motion of God's Spirit. Even the outward events of world history point to God's kingdom; and in any case our inner being is never to be placed on a level with God or seen as a part of God. I am convinced that there is a way to get rid of this conception, which is given new emphasis nowadays and leads in the end to making the soul into the creator of God or into a nascent Christ.

Matt. 6:10

There is, however, only one way. It must be taken seriously that our highest calling is to have personally, in our inmost hearts, a common will with the

---

2 Friedrich Schleiermacher, 1768–1834, *Monologen* (1801), 24..

inmost heart of God. When God enters my innermost being, life comes to me, the all-embracing life of God as the life that has become mine, the life that now I myself may live and must live. The approach of God's kingdom in his mighty, world-embracing history is bound up with the penetration of his Spirit into my heart. Consequently my life is so completely transformed from within to without that, as it goes in the direction of the coming kingdom of the last times, it comes nearer and nearer to it in outward form.

Pascal therefore was right in saying, "Knowledge of the true nature of man, knowledge of his real happiness and true virtue, as well as knowledge of true religion, are inseparably bound together."[3] Before man broke his community with God, God himself was to be found on all the paths of the soul's inner land. And at that time he encountered man in the garden of creation. It was meant to be preserved and built up by the hand and spirit of man for God's kingdom, yes, penetrated in all its parts, named, and mastered as well. Today, the deeper the way leads us into the hiddenmost recesses of the inner land, the more we are bound to come across the recollection of God and the longing for a renewed bond of life with him. It is in these innermost regions that God enters into the soul anew and from there wants to win over and penetrate our whole life. The book of nature, of visible creation, remains our task just as much as the book of history and of history's end – these gifts laid before our eyes and given to us by God through which we can recognize him even though they often seem still sealed with seven seals. Yet nature and its origin,

Rom. 6:4
John 5:24

Luke 17:20–21

Gen. 3:8

Wisd. of Sol. 13:1–9

Rom. 1:19–20

Rev. 5:1

---

3 Blaise Pascal, 1623–1662, *Pensées*, No. 442.

history and the end of history, eternity and infinity, the beyond and the future, the kingdom of God – all these should light up for us not only in an outer way but just as much, and even more, in an inner way.   Ps. 19

From all this, it follows clearly that this book has nothing to do with discussions on psychology and least of all on experimental psychology, which deals with the physical senses. The efforts made by researchers need to be mentioned only where the new psychology of religion and modern psychoanalysis touch on the deepest areas of the life of the soul. In spite of all recent work, the hidden ways into the inner land of our being remain so similar in the most dissimilar people and times, and so hard to describe, that part of the task of this guide must be to recall those precious old tablets set up hundreds and thousands of years ago.[4]

Every great and deep experience must lead to the deepest self-examination. Then, from within, we will be equal to the onslaught of unaccustomed events. The war was a challenge to inwardness in the sense of self-examination because the developments that led up to the war led us further and further away from the roots of all strength. The increasing prosperity of the country and the abundance of work that was achieved were significant outer blessings for which we cannot be thankful enough. But they lose their value entirely and turn immediately into a ruinous curse as soon as they begin, like a top-heavy load, to crush the inner life. With precipitous speed, we are being deprived of the inner blessing of our human calling by the outer blessing of our rapid development. Our

---

4 A reference to the Ten Commandments (Exod. 20:1–17).

public life has lost its human character, and inwardness has been damaged, as a result of the rush and hurry of all the work there is to do on the one hand, and on the other hand by the luxury, excess, and feverishly accelerated pleasure-snatching that has become part of life.

The distress caused by the war can help us forward only if we remember our divine calling, only if instead of haste and excitement we learn to seek the roots of strength again: an inwardness founded in God. Already before the war God awakened spiritual movements in Germany and neighboring countries that wanted to turn away from what is false in our corrupt civilization and seek a more genuine life, which was to be more truthful, more inspired, more inward, human, brotherly, and communal. Since the war, however, the intoxication of a superficial existence has led us again from one injustice to another, from one soulless action to another, from one spiritual murder to another, from death to death.

Without a deep inner uplift at the heart of the people, we will not have the staying power to cope with the effects of war. Without an examination of our hearts in the light of God's kingdom, we will continue to fall prey to new errors, expecting the nation to be lifted up by a human kingdom devoid of God's Spirit.

Matt. 24:6–13

Jesus saw into a time when the earth was to experience the horrors of universal war and bloody revolts, severe privations and plagues. In close connection with these things, he predicted that love would grow cold and lawlessness and injustice would increase. The truth of this prediction has been seen in the

preparations for every war and in those who wage
war. The disturbances of our time now permit the
increase of disorder, lovelessness, and injustice of all
kinds. All the events that have followed the World
War – seemingly only outward events – will develop
into the most terrible judgment that has ever fallen on
humankind. All inwardness will be destroyed if our
love to God grows cold with icy fear for our individual
or collective existence and so-called security. If we no
longer love God and if the glowing love to brothers
and sisters, as well as the radiant energy of love to our
enemies, is drowned because of unchecked sin and the
struggle for material advantage – both so coldly cal-
culating yet so madly passionate – then all inwardness
will perish. Further, it will be the end of all inwardness
if greed for power and violence gain the upper hand
once more; for they are born of hate and are severed
from the depth of the soul, and the Spirit of God at
work in it, and seek only external things, exhausting
themselves in superficialities. And such destruction of   Rom. 14:17
inwardness means destruction altogether.

In the same context in which Jesus spoke about
war among all nations and kingdoms, about lawlessness, and about love growing cold, we hear from him
about enduring to the end, about a movement truly
born of God, about mission, and about the working
of the Spirit throughout the world. In hard times
like these, nothing but a thorough and deep-going
revival of our inner life, nothing but a great and full
awakening to God and to his all-determining rulership, can bring it about that the gospel is carried to
the whole world – the joyful news that Christ alone
matters. For that to happen, however, the life of a

mission church must be given: a life from God that is in keeping with the kingdom of God from its core to the last detail of its outer form, as peace, unity, and community and as love and joy in the Holy Spirit.

This hour of world history is a challenge to inwardness because it means a challenge to be at work in the world, because it implies tasks that are literally boundless. Therefore it is high time that we gather ourselves for serious thought, going deeper and deeper, in order to gain clarity about our inner life. We have to know the foundations and laws of inwardness. Then we will also gain more and more clarity for the whole shaping of life – in what divine order, under what rulership of Christ, and under what decrees of the Holy Spirit we are to set about this shaping of life and how to carry it out. Most of all, it is important that we experience the power of God in our inner being because only then can we be made capable of standing firm and holding out in the storms to come. Only when our inner life is anchored in God can we gain the strength to take up the enormous tasks of the immediate future with the courage of faith. When unity and clarity bring order in our innermost being, then, and only then, can our life attain the warming and radiating power of the light on the lampstand. Then, representing the unity and freedom of the city on the hill, it becomes a light for the whole world.

Matt. 5:14–16

The Inner Life

Inner detachment leads to community

Before the war, the will to power asserted itself in the most diverse forms.[1] It ensnared people in the bustle of outer activity and used up all their energy to increase material possessions. Today again the will to brutal self-assertion and ruthless power expansion lashes our nation and other nations like a raging tempest. This gives a new impetus not only to national independence and to providing work for the unemployed; it also gives a new impetus to collective self-will and personal property and ousts everything else. With increasing unrestraint, the will to live our own life as a nation or as an individual lays claim on our whole being for the upkeep and improvement of our material existence; it is not able to provide a deep inner foundation. On the other hand, a will for the innermost life and for the all-commanding power of God's kingdom as love and justice – a will

---

1 Friedrich Nietzsche, 1844–1900, coined the term *"Der Wille zur Macht"* (the will to power) to describe what he believed to be the main driving force in humans.

Matt. 6:10

for God – forces us into an inner detachment. In this detachment, the solitariness of the soul with God should become a community of two, and then, with

Matt. 18:19–20

his church, become a community of many.

This is why Eckhart (who in many ways knew the inner life as few others have) said: "Nowhere is there perfect peace save in the detached heart. Therefore God would rather be there than in any other being or in any other virtue."[2] This saying, however, is true only when detachment is a separation from the

Eph. 5:11

unfruitful and dead works of darkness, when it leads

Matt. 5:14–16

to the living building up of the city of light. In this city of light, the nature of the kingdom of God will be revealed to everyone as unity in all the diligence and

Acts 2:42–47

courage of the loving works of community. Wherever God is, his kingdom – the final kingdom – draws near. He is the God of peace, whose presence brings freedom from all inner restlessness, all dividedness of

Eph. 2:14–15

heart, and every hostile impulse. However, Eckhart forgets all too easily that the Living God is action just as much as he is peace. His peace is indeed the deepest unity of heart, the harmonious accord of the great diversity of all the gifts and powers of the soul. But on this foundation he brings into being as the goal of his creation an outer unity of all action, a unity that rejoices in every object of love, brings justice into operation for all people, and builds a material world that makes peace a reality on every front through the

1 Thess. 5:14–24

Holy Spirit. God wants to bestow an indestructible harmony upon our inner life, a harmony that shall have an effect outwardly in mighty melodies of love. Power to act results from the energy born of

---

2 Meister Johannes Eckhart, c. 1260–c. 1327, "On Detachment" (Tractate 9 in Pfeiffer's edition).

inner gathering. The gathering of hearts leads to the gathering of a people who show in their industrious work that the kingdom of God is justice, peace, and joy in the Holy Spirit.

Rom. 14:17

With respect to this life-task – this call from Christ – it is important to emphasize once more today that our capacity for work is sure to become exhausted and mechanical, our strength sapped at the core, if no deepening is given to the inner life in stillness and quiet. As soon as inner quiet is lost, the holy springs of the inner world that bring life-giving water to our spiritual life must fail at the very source. Like a man dying of thirst, the overburdened people of today long for their inner life to be strengthened and quickened because they feel how miserably they will die otherwise. The inner strength that comes from the Source and in tranquil silence lets God himself speak and act, leads the believers away from sinking in death to rising in life, to a life that flows outward in streams of creative spirit, without losing itself in externals. This strength as "active stillness" leads believers to work for the world in such a way that they do not become "worldly," and yet they never become inactive.

Ps. 42:2–3

These are times of distress; they do not allow us to retreat just because we are willfully blind to the overwhelming urgency of the tasks that press upon human society. We cannot look for inner detachment in an inner and outer isolation, as implied by Eckhart's sayings (which are liable to be misunderstood, to say the least). We are thankful that the highly mechanized nature of world economics today does not allow this pious selfishness anymore, for it gives

us more protection from self-deception than we had
in earlier times. But the lack of vital and effective
action shows us when our striving after detachment
has not penetrated to the inmost springs of creative
power. Where this power is at work in us, there is a
detachment that is a thorough letting go of self and
therefore a freedom for the hardest work; this gathers
believing people into the most living kind of community. Their love to all people now presses forward out
of all isolation to the ends of the earth, and yet they
will never be able to give up the common gathering at
the focal point of strength.

To those who are responsible in their consciences,
the only thing that could justify withdrawing into
their inner selves to escape today's confusing, hectic
whirl would be that their fruitfulness is enriched by
it. It is a question of gaining within, through unity
with the eternal powers, that strength of character
which is ready to be tested in the stream of the world,
the strength that alone can cope with the demands
of this age. Not flight but gathering for attack is
the watchword. We must never withdraw from the
rushing stream of present-day life into a selfishness
of soul that makes our love grow cold in the face of
need and the countless paths of guilt connected with
it. Our detachment, turned into coldness of heart,
would then reach such a height of injustice that it
would exceed the injustice of the world. Unless we
share the distress and guilt of the world, we fall prey
to untruthfulness and lifelessness, to eternal and
temporal death. And those who are prepared to share
only the inner need of others, and not their outer
need as well, fully and completely, are cutting life into

2 Cor. 4:16–18

James 2:13–17

Matt. 25:35–46

halves. They are thereby losing the inner half of life, the very part they were supposed to be gaining or preserving. For they have forgotten Jesus Christ, who took on outer need just as much as inner need: in his eyes the two are inseparably one. It is possible to share lovingly and militantly in the life of our times only when we respond with every fiber of our being to the work demanded, when in every drop of our heart's blood we feel the distress, and want to share in suffering it and thereby in actively overcoming it. It is in quietness that we find the way to give this help.

Matt. 9:4–7

Gal. 6:2

The kingdom of God within

Jean Paul[3] describes a raging tempest in which the surface of the water is broken up in jagged and foaming confusion while the sun still shines on it, without being hidden by turbulent clouds. The mirror of our feelings also cannot help becoming stormy and agitated sometimes with all the seething activity in which we are obliged to live and carry on our work. Yet our hearts know of a heaven with a sun that in radiant quiet preserves an untouched and inviolable strength. This heaven is the rising sun of God's approaching reign. Jesus Christ, the morning star of the future, not only proclaimed it to us; he also brought it close to us in his life and death, in his word and deed. The following words of Fichte will be understood by anyone who sees this heaven: "Do you wish to see God face to face as he himself is? Do not look for him beyond the clouds; you can find him everywhere, wherever you are." The kingdom of God draws near over all the earth. God is near wherever a

Rev. 22:16

Matt. 5:8

---

3 Jean Paul Friedrich Richter, 1766–1825.

complete reversal of all things is sought – the reversal that brings his rule with it. His kingdom has no territorial boundaries.

We are not Christians (in the only sense in which it is possible to be Christians – in the inner sense that affects all outward things as well) until we have experienced in our own hearts these decisive words about the presence of Christ:

> The righteousness based on faith says, Do not say in your heart, "Who will ascend into heaven?" (that is, to bring Christ down) or "Who will descend into the abyss?" (that is, to bring Christ up from the dead). But what does it say? The word is near you, on your lips and in your heart.

Rom. 10:6–8

The Word comes into our hearts because it has come into the world. The eternal Word became temporal flesh; God's Son became the Son of Man. Every time what you do is done sincerely, believed wholeheartedly, and confessed openly, the Word becomes again body and flesh in your mouth, in your heart, in the work of the believing church, in the loving, active community that is its organism. It is through the Holy Spirit that this comes about, just as it did when the Son came for the first time. In order to penetrate the life of humankind, the Word goes to our inmost hearts again and again. The kingdom has no time boundaries.

1 Thess. 2:13

John 1:1–14

No eye can see light apart from itself, but only in itself. Light comes from outside, and its rays illuminate the inside. God's morning star, his rising sun, draws near to us from the other world. When we believe this fact and when this news reaches our

2 Pet. 1:19

inmost life, the morning star has arisen in our hearts.
We are filled with light because the Light of the
World has reached us from afar. So he gives light to
every person who comes into this world. Seeing takes
place only when the eye receives light rays in its own
deepest depths. "Therefore you cannot grasp God
apart from yourself. He himself must let the rays of
his Spirit pierce deep into the depths of your heart
to stamp his image there in order that you may know
him." In Jesus, the image of God has appeared so
clearly and so undeniably that from now on it is from
him that we receive our calling into our hearts. The
image of God that Jesus brings to us is love: love as
the will to unity. We are called to be images of God,
and through this calling his Spirit wants to rule all
people and all things and form them into one united
whole. The kingdom has no subjective boundaries.

John 12:35–46

Matt. 6:22

Ps. 36:9

Col. 2:9

John 14:8–10

John 17:11, 21

We see God directly before our inmost heart as
soon as the light is no longer eclipsed by all the busy-
ness of our ego as it obstinately pushes its way to the
fore. God shows himself to us as the beaming sun
that alone can bring abiding life. He brings in the new
day, his day that brings judgment on the dark life of
self. He seeks to bring all people into redeeming light
and unite them under his rulership. We find the focal
point of our inner life in God, the central sun of our
existence, because in him we recognize the central
fire of all creation, of history, and of the history of the
last things. Without him, collectedness of spirit in
the depths of our soul will be cast to the winds again
and again. Only through our becoming one with God
in the depths of our being will it become possible. A
battle can be won only when the field marshal and

John 3:19, 21

his staff keep completely calm in the midst of all the turmoil. Similarly, we are able to cope with the demands of today's need and distress only when we have found an inner collectedness in God. And we shall find this only when lightning from the kingdom of God has struck and lit up the whole horizon.

Every bit of life must have a center somewhere deep inside it. Just as the earth without its glowing center would be no less dead than the moon, just as the inner core contains the life-strength of the fruit, just as a flower's beautiful petal-cups shield the organs of fertilization, in the same way there can be only one center for all life-energy: the hidden and the inner. The power of God's kingdom lies hidden in its innermost core, in the heart of God. It comes to light in Jesus, the hidden focus of all history. Jesus reveals this power at the very heart of faith to the simple

Matt. 11:25 and to children. It remains hidden from the wise and clever because only the childlike heart is able to grasp the plan of love. The only way our soul can know God and be known by him is for us to become one in our own inner depths with the center of all worlds and all life in them. The inmost core decides between life and death.

Therefore, the most dangerous sickening of life does not halt at the external forms of life but proceeds with its decay and destruction to attack

Eph. 4:18 the innermost core. In fact, life could not really be affected by sickness if the core of our being were to remain untouched by it. We are sick, and we do fall prey to death, because we have become estranged from the fire that is the core of all life, the core

Gal. 4:9 of all that takes place. In this state of sickness we

understand nothing of God's judgment in his history.
Through this sickening, our inner eye is blinded   2 Cor. 4:4
so that it cannot see the kingdom of God. Every   John 11:10
weakening of inwardness strikes at the source of
our life-power. Every strengthening of our outward
existence that is won at the expense of inwardness
squanders our vital strength and endangers our
inner existence. Only wealth of life gathered in the
innermost depths makes us capable of that quality of
generosity which finds its happiness in giving. The
innermost core of God's kingdom is the surrendering
love and active sacrifice of the pure life.   Eph. 5:2

In the same way, it is in the innermost core of our
life that the love of the sacrificed Christ kindles the
rich fire of renunciation, a letting go and surrendering of everything that is given us in the way of
personal abilities and possessions. Every impoverish-   Matt. 10:39
ment and sickening of our inner being means a loss of
warmth and depth, a loss that shows up plainly in all
our efforts and activities. Every healing of the inner
life leads to loving sacrifice, that is, to purer and more
vigorous action.

The hypocrisy of outward piety

Jesus has wielded the sword of speech more powerfully than anyone else against the danger that
religion, our inmost treasure, becomes outward
form. No one has stressed more than he did the vital   Luke 11:37–44
importance of the actual state of a person's inner
life. Because he is the heart of God, he brought the
kingdom of God, and this kingdom seeks to gain
authority over all things by touching hearts and
changing everything, starting with the heart. That   Luke 17:20–21

is why he seeks the inner life of all people. We know
from him that even the most untruthful person, even
the person who is furthest from God, has an inner
being. God seeks with all the means of judgment and
love to move the heart of each person: he wants the
approach of his day, just as much as the effect of his
love, to bring each one to look in his own heart and
turn around. In this way, everything will be changed
by being overthrown and set up new. And he sees our
hearts as they are. All purifying or whitewashing of
externals is in vain. "Inwardly you are full of hypocrisy and lawlessness." "Inwardly they are full of greed
and self-indulgence, full of dead men's bones and all
kinds of rottenness." Jesus hates the outward appearance of piety and holiness when the heart dishonestly
boasts of spiritual values it does not possess and sinks
further and further away from God. He himself said
the most serious thing that can be said about this:
"This people draws near to me with their mouths
and honors me with their lips, but their hearts are far
removed from me, and they serve me in vain because
they teach teachings that are nothing but the commandments of men."

As a result of the war and the shock and collapse
that followed, people should feel that God wants to
use the heavy burden of our times to bring them to
examine themselves. Again it is all-important that
it is not with our mouths only that we promise to
change, and not with our lips only that we honor the
Ruler to whom alone all power is given. The will of
the heart must be turned into deed if it is serious and
sincere. Sincerity is decisive. Through the judgment
of his earnest love God wants to bring about a real

John 3:16

Mark 1:15

Ps. 139:23–24

Matt. 23:25–33

Isa. 29:13

Matt. 7:24

transformation in all who are ready for it – a change of heart, a change in actual inner condition, and with that a change in their whole attitude to life.

Rom. 2:4

The darkness of the human heart

What glimpses into the dark recesses of the human heart have been afforded by the savagery of the war and the agitation it has stirred up: fear for existence, greed to possess, nationalistic fervor, and revolutionary passions! Our times have once more revealed the state of our inner life: we are filled with everything but God, who alone fulfills our destiny. And yet we still deceive ourselves.

People speak of dedication and sacrifice of life – their devotion unto death for the sake of brothers, friends, comrades, the homeland, freedom, or justice. What they mean by all this is the killing and plundering of all those they look upon as enemies of these things so precious to them. Just this is what makes Jesus give such a strong warning about those who come in sheep's clothing, "but inwardly they are ravening wolves"! Their hearts are set on plunder and destruction because the essence of sin – unbroken self-seeking – rules in them as much as ever in spite of all Christian disguises and in spite of all quasi-prophetic banners of justice. The war and the opportunities for power politics that followed have exposed in an appalling way the gruesome violence with which man's inner being is filled. Truly, man's condition today appears just as in the words of the psalm on which the Letter to the Romans throws so serious a light: "Their heart is destruction," destruction that we prepare for ourselves and others.

Matt. 7:15

Matt. 24:4–5, 24

Rom. 3:10–18

Ps. 5:9

Like the fate of countries devastated by the World War, people's inner being today can be compared to a deep mountain ravine: dark shadows of judgment are spread over it. Only withered trunks and bony roots betray to a discerning eye the fact that death did not always rule here. The water that used to be the life of this valley has been blocked. Stones and boulders fill the ravine and seem to have buried every hope. The deeper and more truthfully we see into the actual condition of our inner life, the more hopeless and desperate our fate seems to us. What amazement must have filled the Samaritan woman when the infallible mouth of the Messiah declared that her buried inner life was to be completely renewed and

John 4:7–10   filled forever with fresh strength and rich content! There is a life-giving water that today, too, transforms the darkest abyss or the most awful desolation into a place of joy and surging life. It is the Spirit of him who said: "The water I shall give them will become

John 4:14   in them a spring of water welling up to eternal life." From this deepest of all springs even the uttermost devastation that has come upon lands and peoples shall be transformed everywhere into a region and people filled with far-reaching peace, a place where the powers of God's future world shall be poured out

Isa. 32:15–20   through the Holy Spirit.

God does not want our inner self to remain bleak

Ezek. 18:23   and desolate – a dark abyss. He is able to change the storms of his judgment, which threaten the terrified soul, into the sunshine of undeserved love. He wants to bring peace and clarity to the heart where until now disruption and darkness have reigned. God's day of judgment threatens to smash

conquered and unconquered nations alike, yes, the
entire mammonistic world economy. But once we
renounce the kingdom of mammon, murder, lying,
and impurity in order to belong from then on to the
kingdom of God, his day of judgment, the day of the
Lord, will become the day of *salvation*.

2 Pet. 3:10–14

The struggle within every heart
God knows how the inner fight goes on with deep
pain in the hidden recesses of the heart. He knows
that the conscience lives there, bringing its witness
again and again to the heart's awareness. He knows
the hidden thoughts, how they accuse and excuse
each other. He knows how many people wrestle in
vain with inner ties that bind them to what is base.
He knows with what lying power false demonic ideals
and idols try to assert themselves. He knows that the
ravening beast of prey confuses the conscience in the
guise of an angel of light and so-called liberation.

Rom. 2:15–16

Rom. 7:15–25

John 8:44

2 Cor. 11:14–15

The inward person delights in God's Law. We
would so gladly live according to it. At the same time,
along with the demands made by God's justice, other
claims stir our inmost being – the claims of our own
life, of our nation, or of the oppressed classes. We
would like to be free for God's justice in both the
inner life and outer circumstances. And we cannot.
The Spirit draws us toward the heavenly city of God's
church and God's kingdom. But we are bound by the
heavy weight of the iron-fisted autonomy of those
other things – bound to the earthly cities of human
community and human sovereignty and their bloody
interests. God knows that all nations and all people
live in this inner struggle. For God has written the

Ps 1:2

Gal. 5:16–18, 25

Rom. 1:18–21 Book of the Law on the hearts of even the remotest nations. Only he, and whoever is in unity with him in the all-discerning Spirit, can judge and discern the hidden depths of man. The Father sees into what is hidden. He delights in the truth that is within the heart. He wants to teach us to know the truth in the Ps. 51:6 hidden depths, in the innermost recesses of the heart. And only God's pure truth in his perfect love, as it John 1:14, 17 took shape in Jesus and his first church, has the power Rom. 1:18–21 to set us free. Everything else is lying and deceit.

The blocked stream

The fate of the countries so hard hit today brings to mind a remarkable story about a remote, parched valley, whose impoverished inhabitants vaguely remembered a time when it had been different and better. Once upon a time, a life-giving mountain stream had flowed there and brought wealth and happiness to the valley. But guilt, in which all who lived there had a share, had ruined everything; the great mountains began to move. Huge boulders plunged into the valley. It seemed as though absolutely everything was about to be buried under the debris. Neither buildings nor rows of houses were any protection. Then the hurtling masses of rock stopped. They halted in front of the houses. But the river was blocked. The life that had flourished seemed destroyed forever. Poverty and distress began their rule. Even memories of the past began to fade slowly away.

But a son of the valley grew up, despised by the others, who was moved by the fate of his people. Day and night he thought about delivering them, ready to attempt it. He knew about the stream and where it was blocked. He accomplished the colossal task, moving the mountainous weight of rocks; but as he moved the last boulder, letting the water flow once more into the valley, he, the savior of his people, was buried under it. Yet he rose to life again, this man who had risked his life for their sake. He ruled forevermore over his people, who had had everything given back to them.

Acts 2:24, 33

It is Jesus who has moved the boulder of our mountainously heavy guilt so that the river of life can flow unhindered into our inner being. As Lord over our innermost being, Jesus brings riches and happiness to our inner life. And just as he healed the bodies of the sick and possessed, also now in this relentless catastrophe of world history he wants to set free the buried bodies and ruined workplaces and make a new life possible in his land. Our hearts cannot be set free from the deadening pressure of hidden sin until his liberating action, given as his gift, gains room in our innermost being. And when this experience has become ours, the essential thing is to allow him to take command and have more and more authority.

Rev. 21:6

Rom. 3:23–25

Rom. 5:20

Rom. 6:13

When his kingdom comes to us in this way, we live from within according to the spiritual laws of his kingdom, also in our work and in the communal order of our life. Even the outer shape of our life shall be in accord with the kingdom of God as his prophets portrayed it. When his word rules in us, when his nature unfolds in us, it is wealth of life undreamed of, which floods the parched depths of our inner being and pours forth from there into the world outside as living, active love. In place of the cloud of judgment that threatens everything comes the superabundant light of his revelation. This light shows the living way.

Already today, the church of faith and love gains the possibility of judging and ordering the innermost as well as the outermost details of life according to the justice, peace, and joy of his kingdom.

Gal. 5:22

In this light, the somber darkness of the World War with all its causes and consequences is revealed as that guilt which in many people causes the river of life to be blocked. Many forgot that Jesus is life. Because they sought life in other waters, everything had to be buried. God let this war come over us like a heavy landslide because it is his will to give inner help through such radical intervention. But it turns out as the Revelation of John foretold about the last times: "And those that remained, who were not killed by these plagues, still did not repent of the work of their hands. Neither did they repent of their manifold murders. Indeed, they blasphemed God in heaven instead of repenting of their deeds."

Rev. 16:11

Rev. 9:20–23

Untold numbers turn sharply away from the way of Jesus. They seek out the way of idols so that they can continue to worship mammon all the more zealously – mammon, the murderer from the beginning, the father of lies, the prince of impure spirits. They endeavor to make themselves strong through impure streams of racial ties instead of at long last looking for the one pure spring. Through collapse on all sides, we are directed more earnestly than ever before to the one who took upon himself our poverty and distress to make us pure and strong in his Spirit. Every single person should have recognized at long last that no human, self-made effort can bring peace and life to the earth. Only the sovereign reign of God can do this. In the midst of the serious situation today, God himself wants to be the Savior and helper in our inner life and

Isa. 53:4–5

John 16:33

in every area of our life. There is only one gospel for
all creation, one and the same gospel for everyone, for
every class of people, and for every tribe and nation.
Whoever represents a different gospel for himself, his
nation, or his class brings a curse with him.

Gal. 1:6–8
2 Cor. 11:4–15

God alone renews our hearts
The reality of God is proved by the fact that he brings
about the renewal and strengthening of our hearts
that we cannot find without him. The unity of Jesus
with the Father is the living reality of his divine
sonship and the same as the unity of God and Christ
with the Holy Spirit. This unity shows itself in our
innermost life. For there his Spirit works the powerful
religious and moral transformation that could never
be attained without him. He is unity in himself and
in us. Therefore his Spirit can represent and spread
only unity and peace, also in outer life. He knows of
only one way and one leadership. Jesus Christ, who is
Lord and Spirit, goes no roundabout way and knows
no separate mediator.

John 14:6, 20–23

1 Tim. 2:5

God gives himself in the certainty of direct
contact. In him alone does the heart's need for
security find the firm ground of the here and now,
for which it must long continually. The presence
of Christ is the wonderful gift of God in which we
receive perfect unity with God in love and faith.
Through this experience, however, the stark difference between his purity and our guilt dawns on us
just as powerfully. We stand in the midst of disunity
between people, classes, and nations, while he is and
remains unity. It is precisely in this complete oneness
that we become aware of the abysmal difference that
separates our nature from his.

John 5:24

Gal. 2:20

The writings of the apostles call this experience
the illumination of our hearts by God. It brings the
brightness of his glory into our inner being. God
shines in Christ and in his countenance. Illuminated
by the presence of God, the hidden recesses of the
heart are revealed, so that we have to cast ourselves
down and worship him. We are overpowered by the
fact that the light of his incomprehensibly glorious
nature makes us feel all the more deeply the darkness
of our own being. If we accept the life of Jesus with
his unmistakable words and deeds, if we accept them
unadulterated and without any devious interpreta-
tions, our entire life, private and public, will be
revealed as utterly opposed and hostile to him.

Only in Jesus can our inner being find happiness
and inmost satisfaction: nothing else corresponds
to what our innermost being is and should be, in the
light of its origin. Only when our life is hidden with
Christ in God do we experience our real, unique
destiny, which without him has to remain buried in
the dark. This destiny is to be God's image: to rule
in his Spirit over everything through love and love's
creative power. The more we experience his wealth
of life, the more we long with all our heart to grow in
this inner experience and this creative shaping of life.
For the experience of God's gifts and the knowledge
of his divine rulership over everything can never
reach a conclusion in this life. It needs to be renewed
every day.

The great commotion in the world today makes
it more and more urgent to gain inner strength in
quiet encounter with Christ. This will make it possible for us to remain under the rule of his authority.
Since we are situated in the midst of such a terribly

Eph. 1:18
2 Cor. 4:6
Eph. 5:13
1 Cor. 14:25

Eph. 4:1–6

Col. 3:1–3

2 Pet. 3:18

John 15:4–5

unpeaceful world, we need constant nourishment
for our inner life. It is important to look toward and   John 6:48–51
think about that which is above external things and
in direct contrast to the outward form they take
today. Instead of following the weak and alien spirits
of hate and of violence, of lying and of impure, greedy
possessiveness, we are allowed to follow the one Spirit
who alone is stronger than all other spirits. Only the
strongest power of inner resistance can prevent our
inner life from being buried by what is happening   Eph. 6:11–13
around us now on the earth.   1 Pet. 5:8–9

Without a rebirth in our hearts, we will glean
from fluctuating world events either a false
meaning – based perhaps only on material consider-
ations or on emotional or racial ties – or no meaning
at all. The course of history is interpreted falsely by
many people in the interests of their own nation,
for example, or their own society. For most people,
though, it never has any meaning at all. There is
only *one* possible way of bringing this confusion to
an end. One's whole person and the whole of one's
life must undergo a complete about-face toward the
kingdom of God. Rebirth is the only name we can   Matt. 6:33
give to such a radical change with its childlike trust   Rom. 6:13
in God's intervention and firm, manly expectation of
it. This is the complete opposite of the former life. It   Luke 18:17
is only through such a complete change that we – by
going through judgment – can recognize in all that
happens the approach and intervention of God's rule.
We can never see the kingdom of God or have any
part in it without a rebirth of heart that breaks down
the whole structure of our life and then makes a new
start, a completely different one. Only a new begin-   John 3:3, 5
ning that starts from the very bottom in the process

of becoming a true person, only the rebirth that starts
Matt. 18:3 at the very beginning, is able to prepare us for the
kingdom of God. It must be a new beginning of our
whole personal life.

Consequently, it is only through the Spirit who
embraces all the powers of the future kingdom of
God that this can happen. Only the Spirit of the
kingdom of God can put a seal on the passport
without which the door into this kingdom remains
shut – the passport to God's kingdom, which is meant
to confirm that we already now live in the Spirit and
Eph. 1:13 in the order of the final kingdom. But just as a tiny,
newborn baby is far from being able to master life,
so too the rebirth brought about by the Holy Spirit is
neither more nor less than the beginning of new life,
1 Pet. 2:2 which still needs to be strengthened and completed.
For us weak people, however, this is possible only as
a slow process of being made fit for God's kingdom
Heb. 5:12–14 and his righteousness. Even after rebirth has given
the first glimpse into the kingdom of God, our hearts
still remain subject to the old inhibitions and restric-
tions epitomized as "flesh" by Paul, that methodical
thinker of early Christian times. He testified of
himself explicitly that his flesh had no peace, not only
because of struggles from without but just as much
2 Cor. 7:5 because of fears from within.

Strength to overcome

What is incomplete in our existence gives the
believer a powerful incentive to deepen his inner life
Phil 3:12 constantly. It is of the utmost importance that in
these serious and extremely menacing days we gain
a growing clarity about our inner life. We must not

let our emotional nature deceive our hearts in these agitated times. Even when it has been touched by the Holy Spirit, our excitable inner nature remains weak. Our hearts are flooded as the blood circulates; our emotional life flows in this bloodstream and often continues as long as we live to be determined by its urges and feelings.

If those around us are gripped and swept up by the excitement in their blood, we often fall prey to it too, because we are not able to put up a true resistance born of the Spirit. The distress of our own class or our own nation has a particularly strong effect on us. Mass suggestion used by great national movements appeals to our blood ties and class solidarity and often works so decisively on us that we utterly forget the call to the kingdom of God and his Spirit, or we completely falsify it. Even if we continue to profess him, emotional ties and fear for existence have driven the Spirit away from us. In order to face all fears, and still more, in order to resist all the impure and bloody raptures of fanaticism, our consciences need a healing that steadily gains ground. This healing can come about solely through the holy, all-loving, utterly pure, and completely true Spirit, the Spirit of Jesus Christ, who unites all good in himself. His objectivity is sober and clear.

No experience, however agitating, and no shock, however violent or bitter, must be allowed to sweep past without this result: that the rule of Christ in us gains ground in our hearts and in our whole life. The aim of his rule is to fill our inner life with an objective clarity that cannot be shattered by any force of circumstance. His Word and his Spirit want

Luke 23:21–23

Matt. 13:22

to work in us uninterruptedly as his instruments in order to make us strong in every battle and capable of the hardest work. The blessing of everything good shall conduct us so firmly and clearly on the way of Jesus Christ – the way that leads straight ahead – that neither successes nor failures in the world can make us swerve into false ways.

We have to follow the same way as Jesus; we must follow it just as Jesus did. Then no seductive call will divert us from this mission, which he left to us as his mission. In just the same way as the Father sent him into the world, he sends us: in just the same way, with the same stand in life, completely free from adulteration by other elements! Only in this way will our life be fruitful. He wants all our gifts to come to life and unfold in order to equip us for the new tasks of the changing world situation. The rulership of Christ denotes strength for the inner life through inner gathering and consecration, and through this, through this alone, also strength for an outer life with a living influence in the right work or occupation.

To become strong in our inner being can mean only one thing: that Christ lives in our hearts through faith because we are being grounded and rooted in love. We need Christ all the time in our inner being, the Christ who was crucified for us, the Christ who is alive for us. He invades us with his fullness, with all the fullness of God, which wants to pour itself over all spheres of our activity as the supreme authority of love. God is love. Only he who remains in love remains in God and God in him. God's rulership is the kingdom of love. Love is his justice. Because his kingdom knows no frontiers, his Messiah-King has

Matt. 16:24

John 20:21

John 17:18

Eph. 3:16, 19

Col. 2:9–10

1 John 4:16

put the love of God to friend and foe into our hearts. Luke 6:27–31
It is poured into our hearts through the Holy Spirit. Rom. 6:13
  Whoever betrays this by shutting out love to his
opponents or to enemies of his class or nation drives
away the Holy Spirit and delivers up his heart to
deceptive spirits. Love wants to flood our private
as well as our public life and rule over it in such a
way that there can be no rival authority. Paul prays Phil. 1:9–11
for this for all people because it is the true and the
only strengthening for our inner being. In our inner
life we need an experience of Christ that transcends
all knowledge. This means that as king of the final
kingdom he rules over our lives already here and now
in exactly the same way as he will in his final kingdom. Matt. 6:10
  We need men of prayer who, like Paul, bend their
knees and lift hands that are unstained with blood 1 Tim. 2:8
or any kind of impurity so that through the Spirit of
God the believers may be strengthened powerfully
in their inmost being – strengthened in their whole
attitude to life. We need to be reminded daily that
inwardly we must be renewed from day to day even
if the body perishes in hunger, distress, and misery
or is carried off and destroyed by persecution and
death for the sake of truth. If in the storm of public 2 Cor. 4:16
opinion and the towering waves of chaos, we want to
keep a clear, firm course instead of inwardly suffering Rom. 12:12
shipwreck – then our hidden inner being needs daily Col. 4:2
the quiet haven of communion with God. Matt. 6:6

The Heart

The heart contains unknown riches
The World War brought a time of sharp testing and deep affliction. It has tested our endurance to its very limits, bringing in its train loss of national wealth and disruption of world economy, unemployment and impoverishment, mutual hostility and untold ills that shatter public confidence. Even the most indifferent must feel that whether they will pass the test or not depends on what their hearts are able to bear. Those who previously had nothing but a smile for demands made by the inner life now feel how important it is that their hearts are firm. The "morale of the troops," the confidence of a people, the solidarity of classes, the faithfulness of true community, like that of individuals, are a measure of the heart's energy to hold all good powers together and to ward off all destructive ones. We need the inmost strength of stout hearts in order to be able to bear the consequence of war or world crisis without permanent injury.

Suffering is an appeal to our hearts. It forces us to be on the watch for ways of finding the necessary strength and courage, because the heart affects the whole person. Being the inmost core, the heart means more than anything else not only for the spirit, but just as much for the body. Even physical capacity depends on strength of heart. No feeling, thought, or motion of the will is without influence on the body. Ovid recognized this even in those ancient days: "Even in the human body, the heart counts more than the hand; the strength that gives the body life is in the heart."[1] Life radiates from the heart and preserves the center of its strength in this innermost core. The outer body perishes. The heart decides between life and death, for it is so closely linked with the soul and is meant to be so open to the spirit that it can and should have everlasting life.

Prov. 4:23

People who are guided by superficialities cannot stand up to any hard trial. They have too feeble a concept of what wealth of life and strength can fill the heart. The most important things in life are lost to them. Only events that have a powerful outer effect give them some idea of what power the inner life can have. The great, wide mouth of a mighty river once showed Columbus what riches must lie hidden in the interior behind the newly discovered coast. This coast could not possibly be mistaken any longer for the edge of a small island. And no one could possibly remain indifferent to the heart of a continent! The sun that shone over it was indeed familiar. Clouds could indeed be seen gathering over it. No one could from then on be satisfied with the outside edge, however – the beach strewn with shells and wreckage and pounded monotonously by the sea of the world

---

1 Ovid, *Metamorphosis*, XIII.

outside. The discoverers could not rest until the
unfathomable wealth of the interior lay before their
astonished eyes.

The whole world shall recognize, by the stream
of light radiating from the seven lampstands, what a   Rev. 1:12–13
land of light, what a part of God's kingdom is given
to the church of Jesus Christ. The city of God as the
city on the hill shall be visible to all lands far and   Matt. 5:14
wide so that all seeking people may have a longing to   Ps. 22:27
know the center of its inner life, the inner secret of its
free citizenship and its church unity. All people over
all the earth shall ask about the citizenship of the
kingdom of God, about his embassy here and now,   2 Cor. 5:20
and about the future order it represents. They must   Heb. 12:22–23
recognize one thing above all, that they must become
one with the heart of this church and city of God   Eph. 2:12–22
before they can enter its gates.   Rev. 22:14

The most recent world history shows us that
neither foreign rule nor home rule will come to any
good unless the heart of a country is won, for all
wealth lies hidden within. Whoever does not learn to
understand the heart of God in Jesus Christ, whoever
will not begin to journey through all the outlying
regions of God's world rule to the very center in
order to become one with the ultimate will of God's
heart, whoever does not seek the Holy of Holies, will
never understand that God wants only one thing. He
will never understand that in spite of the fact that
in history God has appointed the secular state – a
power of bloodshed and diplomacy that is anchored
in the right to property – God wants only one thing
in the end: love without violence, freedom from all
possessions and property rights, simple truthfulness

and brotherly justice, community of all people everywhere without self-interest and property – that is, the kingdom and the church. Whoever keeps his or her back turned on the heart of God will be just as perplexed when confronted by the mystery of the human heart. For that is where the likeness of God shall be revealed. Such people will never be able to grasp

> The greatest wonder in all creation,
> Of time and space the masterpiece:
> The heart of man with its elation,
> The heart with all its ecstasies.[2]

The Bible, which speaks of the heart in such a rich and profound way, is of all books the only one that can satisfy the inner life and fill the heart. If it is not seen superficially according to its letter but deeply in its heart and soul, it witnesses everywhere to the heart as the innermost mystery. It even goes so far as using the Hebrew expressions for "heart" and for "that which is within" as synonyms. In the Bible the heart is the antithesis of superficiality and pretense. What penetrates to the inmost depths does not simply stay on the surface. What comes from the inmost depths is the noblest and sincerest of all. If a man's heart is corrupt, nothing he touches remains incorrupt. But the outer life resists the inner life and strives against it. Only seldom is there harmony between them.

Luke 24:32

2 Tim. 3:15–17

Matt. 23:25–28

Matt. 12:35

Gal. 5:17

Rom. 7:23

A corrupt heart hides behind lies

A pure, creative spirit expresses what is within very clearly and intelligibly by outward and visible signs.

---

2 George Philipp Schmidt von Lübeck, 1766–1849, "*Das Menschenherz*" (The Human Heart).

An impure and untruthful spirit, on the other hand, misuses the outward expression to falsify the true state of affairs. Then the outward appearance is only there to hide what is within, as public economy and politics reveal so painfully in war and in peace. We in our days have had to look on with horror while spirits who have fallen prey to hate and hostility, of whatever party or nation, have practiced the most hateful misuse of the spoken, written, and printed word. They all, every one of them, practice it to this day, dishonestly exaggerating and inventing failures and mistakes in the enemy's camp, and, just as much, exaggerating and inventing advantages and elements of truth in the home camp. Every honest person must be warned of the daily flood of printed matter that bears down on us: *Cave canem!* Beware of the dog! Here you will get barked at and bitten; there is no sense, no understanding, and no insight here because there is no justice. Pass by! Words desecrate the truth! Here the heart is cloaked in lies. 2 Cor. 11:14–15

In the scriptures, the heart is that part of man which is hidden in his inner being. The thought is even intensified by terms like the "inmost" heart and the "depths" of the heart. The secrets of the heart are known to the scriptures. In the scriptures, anyone is marked as unhappy who has to hide himself in an armor of lies and dishonesty because he wants to appear different from what he truly is. Whoever gets entangled in hypocrisy and deceit cannot open up and pour out his heart even before God – the very one who wants to make the heart glad because he loves it and because he wants to give it truth and genuineness. 1 Pet. 3:4 Ps. 44:21 1 Kings 8:39 Deut. 30

Ultimately, however, we cannot hide our innermost being, for we must *do* what is in our hearts. And even if we do not want to admit it, our *deeds* will finally reveal whether our hearts are right

Luke 6:43–45

or wrong. The surprises in this direction that war and postwar times have brought for many should be stamped on our hearts as unforgettable warnings. We must not be indifferent to the abysses that have yawned in front of us: impure and unbridled passions, boundless lies and deceptions, the unrestrained fury of murder and looting, the loveless triumph of ruthless profiteering, the renewed increase of social injustice and oppression, and the deception of class hatred and racism! All of that, and still more, broke out with the most fearsome violence in the war and in the revolution and violent repression that followed it, in inflation, and in the heated political opinions that excited nearly everybody. The shock of these things must be engraved unforgettably on our memory. The dreadful nucleus of these events is something we have to recognize even when it tries to hide behind the glittering armor of the most idealistic words and goals. Not the program but the deed discloses what powers drive the heart and

Gen. 6:5

control it.

All we do is bound to be powerless and evil if the heart is parched and diseased, burdened and faint, or worst of all, if it is hostile, filled with the impure fires

Isa. 1:5

and poisonous smoke of blind hate. Only an inner life that is recollected and that lives in the strength of concentrated peace, only a harmonious heart that does not disintegrate in quarrels and strife, can give proof of strength to act. For only good works are

constructive. Everything else is destructive. We can
see the outward effects, but God tests and knows
the inner recesses of the heart. He wants to lead our
hearts away from murderous demolition to the living
work of building up. He alone knows how to guide
them, just as we guide streams of running water to
one place or another in our gardens. God wants to let
all hearts flow together into *one* great garden, into the
kingdom of his unity, love, and justice, where they all
do what is good because their hearts move them to it
and because the Spirit leads them and urges them on.

In the Bible the heart is seen as crucial in our
renewal. As the Bible sees it, everything of significance is decided in the inner recesses of the heart.
From the heart flow not only the streams of blood
that fill our veins but also the pure winds and waters
of the Spirit. That can be seen in the contrasting
statements about the heart in prophetic and apostolic
writings: not that which enters the heart from
without but that which comes from *within* the heart,
from one's inner being, is what defiles one. It is false
to maintain that one's nature can be influenced by
food taken in by the body or by hygiene or by gymnas-
tics. This is in distinct opposition to the word and life
of Jesus. It results in this thoughtless and deceptive
saying, "You are what you eat," being set up in
opposition to the truth of Jesus. The adherents of this
opinion have themselves had to realize all too often
that the defilement of our inner being lies deeper
than in eating and drinking. The true food, the food
of the Spirit, remains the decisive thing, though, to
be sure, the abuse of eating and drinking through
luxurious living can also burden the heart.

Luke 16:15

Rev. 2:23

1 Sam. 16:7

Isa. 51:3

Ezek. 11:18–19

Mark 7:14–23

Mark 7:2–8

Rom. 14:17

Luke 21:34

In truth it is quite the other way around: a luxurious and voluptuous life has its origin in the heart. What people *are*, they *do*. There are deeper signs of this than diets and rules of hygiene. As long as we think first and foremost of our health and our own wellbeing, we remain unredeemed, with sick and self-seeking hearts. Because we love our life we lose it. Only when we give it up do we find it.

John 12:25

What has vital significance is what comes out of the heart to the light. Every sort of idolatry will inevitably be exposed. The words uttered by the mouth (the outward speech) come from the overflowing of the heart (the inner being). What we *speak about*, we *are* – that is, of course, provided we are speaking from the heart. Nevertheless, the sincerity or insincerity of a person's words cannot be hidden in the long run. A watchful spirit, clearly discerning the spirits, hears the tone of the heart and sees the light of the soul. All empty talk is useless, however lofty the words.

Prov. 26:23–26

Matt. 15:8

The heart is the center of our emotions

What use is all outward service to God if our inner being, our heart, stays at a distance? Only what we do for the Lord with all our heart has any value. What point is there in letting our feet take paths and steps if our hearts do not go along too? All that is done and carried out in imagined strength remains a mere nothing if the living heart does not beat and pulse in it. As long as our heart stays quick and alive, even the weakest people, those least capable of heavy work, can have the strongest influence. The heart is the inner core that does not rest even when the outer body is inactive. God does not look at the outward appearance but at the heart.

Deut. 15:10–15

1 Sam. 16:7

Our strength and our weakness lie in our
innermost being. Our inner attitude, although it can
indeed be hidden or disguised on the outside, nevertheless makes all the difference to our character.
Only that which passes through one heart to another
has any value or strength, because it comes from
the heart. Whoever has experienced how complete   1 Pet. 1:22
or almost complete strangers open their innermost
hearts to one another will feel again and again the
genuine heartbeat in each true word and will turn
away from empty words in which the heart does
not speak.

The living church receives its unity and unanimity
from the continual outpouring of the Spirit. It is there   Acts 2:1–4
that the harmony of all hearts reaches its climax, for
there all have become *one* heart and *one* soul. And   Acts 4:32
this they will be over and over again, every time they   2 Chron. 30:12
believe in the Holy Spirit. Whoever wants to forgive
with his mouth only or preach with his lips only can
give us nothing but disappointment. "A preacher
must have a heart that is on fire before he begins to
preach." With these words, Francis of Assisi revealed
the secret of his fruitful life. "For anything that is to
move hearts must come straight from the heart."³

The heart is rich in strength. What a wealth and
diversity of lively emotions are embedded in the
heart! Many people associate the heart only with
feelings. And indeed, language does not go far wrong
when it speaks so often of the emotional life as the
heart's affair. Our best and deepest feelings are seated
in our innermost being, but just as much so are our
most wicked and harmful ones. All true joy comes   Acts 5:3

---

3 Johann Wolfgang von Goethe, 1749–1832, in *Faust*, Part II, Act 3.

Ps. 16:9
Ps. 28:7 from the heart and fills it with jubilant exultation or quiet happiness. All genuinely good deeds touch the heart. Every joyful hope has its life in the heart. The refreshing of the spirit, and not only that but also the refreshing of the body and soul, is a gift for the inner Ps. 104:15 life, for the heart. For the heart is grateful for every consolation that offers bread and not stones.

The heart really does have to fight against fear and Prov. 12:25 unrest and against pain and sadness. Our times have Ps. 73:21 shown us all too clearly that the heart does not burn Prov. 25:20 only with love and joy. All too often it plunges into the consuming fires of discontent and hate. We must be surprised to the point of being horrified at how for one reason after another passion causes the heart to flare up in rage and distress. What a catastrophe it would be for the heart if it were to exhaust all its Mark 2:6–8 wealth on its conflicting feelings! And how deluding these storms are even though they are often only big enough to fill a teacup! Strong impressions produce shaking emotions. Miserable lusts cramp the heart. Deep emotion alternates with very petty feelings. It can happen that unclarified, unconscious, and sub- Luke 3:15 conscious feelings lead to something good. But often they veil urges that are dangerously apathetic and can lead the heart to destruction.

The heart is the center of thought and attitude
It is not true that the heart can only feel. No, the heart as the inner core of a person is more than feeling: it is intention and will. It is the seat of all deep thoughts, which have meaning only if they move our inner being. "Great thoughts come from the heart."[4]

---

4 Luc de Clapiers, marquis de Vauvenargues, 1715–1747, *Réflexions et maximes* (Reflections and Maxims).

Everything that is great seeks the living core. The
heart is not only inner feeling: it is also inner thought.
There is a speaking and talking going on in the heart
that tries to bring inner clarity to all its thinking.   Prov. 20:5
Reason is not alien to the heart. To be sure, there are
some unreasonable hearts who by their errors show
nothing but folly. But what the sensible and under-   Ps. 14:1
standing heart thinks out is wisdom. It understands   Prov. 2:1–8
how to know and how to recognize the best counsel.   Prov. 14:33
Just in the inconceivably heavy things that the war
and its historical consequences have brought upon us
all, just in the incalculable and unfathomable tasks
that confront us, the heart needs the greatest and
deepest thoughts. These God alone can give.

There are indeed thoughts that will always be
alien to the heart. There are indeed hearts that hate   Matt. 9:4
thinking. But without a certain rich and deep fusion
of thoughts there is no fruitful inner life. The whole
wealth of life intended for the heart is available to
it only when the heart is ready to open itself to the
deepest thinking and reflection. It is in the nature
of the heart to think and reflect. "Your heart is you
yourself. Blessed are you if understanding always
dwells in your heart."[5] Only the consecrated thoughts   Rom. 10:1–10
of a dedicated life lead to this deep understanding.
True understanding is given solely in the thoughts of
God, which turn his will into the holy "thou shalt."   Jer. 29:12–13

The effect that thoughts have on the heart's feelings provides a certain criterion of their value, though
not always an infallible one. As Ruskin expressed
it: "Literature, art, science – they are all fruitless
and worse than fruitless if they do not enable us to

---

5 Friedrich Schiller, 1759–1805, *"Schöner Individualität"* (Lovely
  Individuality).

Isa. 55:8–9

1 Cor. 2:12–14

be glad, and glad of heart at that."⁶ A heart that is
truly alive passes a kind of higher judgment about
those intellectual ideas that cannot fit into our life
at the moment, and perhaps never will. "Like a sun,
the heart goes through our thoughts and on its way
extinguishes one constellation after another!" Jean
Paul saw his inner life before him in this picture. All
knowledge that is related only to the thinking brain
is dead, including mere intellectual knowledge of
biblical things. Such knowledge brings life into deadly
danger unless the heart takes a stand and unless it
is so moved and alive that it is capable of making a
choice between light and darkness, bright and dark

Heb. 3:10

rays, evil stars and good stars. Only thoughts that
have glowing warmth and strength penetrate a pure
heart and stream out from it again. Mirza Schaffy's
search for a completely integrated inwardness comes
to expression when he proclaims:

> Head without heart breeds bad blood;
> Heart without head is still no good.
> For joy and blessing to last forever,
> Heart and head must go together.⁷

This cooperation of two instruments demands an
inner energy that can embrace and hold together
what so often threatens to disintegrate. No heart is
without energy. Yes, the heart is *will*. Just as God's
heart, being love, is the will that gathers and the will
for his kingdom, and just as the heart of Jesus wants
to gather in his outstretched arms everything that is

---

6 John Ruskin, 1819–1900, *The Eagle's Nest*, Section 177 (following a German
   translation).

7 Friedrich von Bodenstedt, 1819–1892, *"Die Lieder des Mirza Schaffy"* (The
   Songs of Mirza Schaffy).

to be united in his church, so the human heart that is
healed in him is the clarified will to gather and unite.   Matt. 23:37
If our inner being is not to let the precious wealth of
truly great thoughts go rushing by, we must have a
heart with a will that is active and glowing, able to
accept words of truth and hold on to them firmly, just   Luke 1:26–38
as Mary did. A will that is weakened by brooding and   Luke 2:51
a nature that is ruled by feelings have never yet been
capable of anything great. Faith received the word of   Matt. 13:15
the Holy Spirit into the heart. This is the only way the   Ps. 119:11
Word can penetrate our life.   Luke 8:15

The ultimate nature of the heart is in fact its inner
desire, and its yet deeper will. This will is able to
comprehend all that is said and to transform it into
dynamic life-values. All intentions and wishes have   1 Sam. 7:3
their root in the heart. There is not only desire in the
heart: deeper than that lie its intentions and resolu-
tions. With its will, the heart holds on to the objects
of its love and devotion. It is the inner disposition, the
deeper direction of will, that makes the character of
the heart what it is. Where a man's treasure is – the
treasure that fills his inner life – there is his heart also.   Matt. 6:21

"There is something in every man's character that
will not let itself be broken, that forms the backbone
of his character."[8] This backbone that is inwardly
so firm and stable is the moral, loving, and uniting
will. Without a decided will there is no character.
"Character is moral order."[9] It is all the elements of
the heart, ordered according to the laws of divine
and human morality, according to the will to unity,
and therefore in the active spirit of pure and warm

---

8 Georg Christoph Lichtenberg, 1742–1799, *Sudelbücher*, Heft G.

9 Ralph Waldo Emerson, 1803–1882, quoted in Samuel Smiles, *Character*.

John 15:10 love. The backbone of this order is the will. As *will*, the heart is the school of character. True, it needs the stream of the world in order to grow strong. The will has to prove itself in work that is a product of active love by helping to build up a life that is consistent with the unity it aims at. It is steeled for this task in the hard struggle against all powers that are opposed 1 Pet. 5:8–9 to unity. But if our will is not rooted in our inmost being, in our heart, we will swim with the stream and Ps. 78:37 cease to have character.

If it is true that character depends on personality, then personality has its life and strength in the inner will. Only in the inmost recesses of the heart does one become truly free. It is only there that a decisive attitude is taken, one that means either moral firmness or a spineless unfreedom. It is the direction the James 1:6 inner attitude takes that makes the personality. As long as this direction seeks nothing but itself, it will lead the personality astray. Personality is "the greatest happiness of earth's children"[10] only when the will no longer seeks itself but comes into action and sets to work for what is greatest of all – God's unity in his Matt. 16:25 kingdom and his church.

Actions reveal one's inner attitude

In the last analysis, it is only in deeds that the Matt. 7:24–27 personality reveals the inner attitude. Only those actions that require the concentration of all the heart's energies can be called deeds. *The* true deed is the uniting of all genuine powers of each individual, bringing togetherness and community to all people: the kingdom of God among them is the concentration

---

10 Johann Wolfgang von Goethe, 1749–1832, "Suleika," in *West-östlicher Divan* (1819).

of all their powers in united deed. Only when we do
not seek our own advantage but that of another are
our deeds in keeping with the powers of God's Spirit
at work in us: when in our deeds we sacrifice our
own life so that community life may be established in
unity, purity, truth, and righteousness.

The greatest deed of the strongest heart was
accomplished by Jesus. When he died on the cross,   Phil. 2:1–8
his resolute determination accomplished it. Here an   2 Cor. 5:15
energy of the will is revealed, a fire of love, a stead-
fastness in carrying out the perfect will, such as can
be found nowhere else. The struggle in Gethsemane   Matt. 26:36–46
and the cry of godforsakenness on the cross give a sig-   Matt. 27:46
nificant glimpse into what willpower was necessary
for the heart of the Son of Man not to be broken by
the anguish of his pain. Yet his love remained strong
and unbroken till the end. In the very torment of
death, the divine life in this heart was marked by will
to unity, consummation of the work of unification,
trust in the Father, prayer for his enemies, concern
for a criminal, tender care for his own, and the com-   Luke 23:34, 43, 46
mending of his spirit into the hands of the Father.   John 19:26–30

Just before that, his high-priestly prayer, as the
most profound speaking of the heart, had once more
proclaimed unity to be the first and last will of Jesus.
"That they all may be *one* as thou, Father, art in me
and I in thee, so that in this, that they are *one*, the
world may know and believe that thou hast sent me!"   John 17:21
The farewell words of Jesus – those words with such
an inexhaustible wealth of thought, spoken to those
who were his disciples in community and mission   John 14–17
work – also revealed the Spirit in this relationship of
unity. This Spirit, the Holy Spirit, was revealed to be

the living representative of Jesus Christ, the advocate of his kingdom and his church, the personal power that thoroughly overwhelms in the conviction that the love that comes from unity is the truth. The Spirit of Truth is the one who calls to mind every word that Jesus said, including his last talks, which prophesy the approaching kingdom of divine unity. The quickening Spirit is the one who communicates the content and form of the future kingdom for us today. Last but not least, the significant symbolism of the Last Supper proclaims the death of Jesus as atonement and liberation; it proclaims his death as the living creation of the new body of Christ, which shall bring the whole of life into perfect unity.

1 Cor. 2:9–10

Matt. 26:26–29
1 Cor. 11:26

All these words and acts show, in a profound wealth of feeling and will, the invincible power of God's thoughts in Jesus Christ, the power to accomplish this deed, the most dynamic deed that ever a heart accomplished. As a revelation of God, this deed of Jesus demonstrates the concentration of all powers on the one goal that is their task. And this goal is nothing more and nothing less than peace, reconciliation, and uniting!

1 John 4:9–10

Eph. 2:14–18

The heart is the inner character. In Jesus it is so firm and clear that in the sacrifice of his life he accomplishes the greatest deed of liberation, uniting, and gathering that can ever be imagined. In Jesus, the accomplished deed reveals his inner perfection. In each of us, the nature of our deeds reveals our heart. Deeds reveal the character of the heart. If it is not clear and undivided, or "single," as Jesus calls it, then the heart is weak, flabby, and indolent, incapable of accepting God's will, of making an important

John 11:51–52

Prov. 20:11

decision, or of taking strong action. That is the
reason why Jesus attached the greatest significance
to singleness of heart, simplicity, unity, solidarity,
and decisiveness. Purity of heart is nothing else than
absolute integrity, which can overcome desires that
enervate and divide. Determined single-heartedness
is what the heart needs in order to be receptive, truthful and upright, confident and brave, firm and strong.

Isa. 1:5

Eph. 6:5–8
Matt. 5:8
Matt. 6:24

Ps. 119:2–3, 10

A divided heart

Yet the Spirit of Jesus is seldom accepted and th e
strength of character that comes from him seldom
achieved. Weakness and dividedness of heart are to
blame. How often the heart tries to overcome its own
cowardice and faintheartedness through cold pride!
The divisive callousness of pride is a weakness that
destroys everything, making the inner self numb and
stubborn, yet torn and disrupted too. The self-will
that splits and divides itself has an arrogance that is
the enemy of the love of God.

2 Chron. 36:15

Rom. 2:5

In vain the heart tries to close itself to the knowledge that it is too weak, too rotten and wicked, too
disunited, too divided, and too hostile to help itself.
For all its blindness to its own nature, and against its
own will, the heart repeatedly has to uncover pride
and arrogance, wickedness and cunning, ruthlessness
and deceit, as the self-will and self-interest that continually divide it. Derangement of the heart can go
so far in rigid obstinacy that all pretense comes to an
end: God is tempted and cursed until darkness fills
the heart's inmost recesses.

Mark 7:21–23

The heart, however, longs for the opposite – for
a development of the inner life that leads to honest

2 Chron. 32:26
Ps. 131:1
Eph. 4:1–4
2 Kings 22:19
Isa. 57:15–16

self-recognition, single-hearted simplicity, and unfeigned humility. In this spirit of modesty, the consciousness of one's own smallness unites with the divine call to true greatness. Such a development, which is brought about by God, requires a penetrating insight into everything that is base in one's own heart, an insight that in fact means a revolution in the heart. No one has an innocent heart when faced with this radical revolution.

Consciousness of guilt and unfulfilled longing for God, however, may not only soften the heart but positively tear it apart and crush it. Many people have shattering things to say about the consuming fire of this longing of the heart. Many call it the deepest thing in them, the thing they want to gain a glimpse into.

> In my heart there burns an eternal lamp,
> quiet and steady;
> only once in a while it flares up high,
> rises to a flame,
> to a blazing fire
> that rages and consumes and destroys –
> then I summon all my energy,
> only one wish have I then,
> only one hope,
> only one thought———.
> And the eternal flame flickers and smokes
> for a long, long time
> until it is appeased and becomes quiet:
> my eternal longing![11]

The blazing flame of longing is certainly there, but it will have to flicker, restless and unappeased, and remain impure unless the heart submits to the

---

11 Michal Grabowski, 1805–1863, a Polish educator.

inner influence of the sharp, clarifying Word and
the cutting wind of the Spirit of God. Then the
impure blaze can give way to the perfect light of the
"Christ in us." Nevertheless, the heart is as weak as
it is obstinate and only too used to its own divided
and disrupted state, and it will not surrender lightly.
It tries by every possible means to defend itself. It
tries passionately to cling to self-chosen, human
ideals, meant to bolster its self-will and hostile
self-assertion – either alone or in community with
kindred hearts who are equally selfish. But it is all in
vain, even though the heart can cover up or postpone
the decisive battle for a long time.

Heb. 4:12–13
Matt. 5:8
Rom. 8:1–2, 10
Gal. 2:20
Jer. 17:9

All mistaken attempts to lift the heart up in human,
emotional "enthusiasm" for some god other than the
Father of Jesus Christ have proved vain. In spite of
every effort, all that the natural state of the human
heart reveals is how far it has fallen away from God.
Today more than ever this is unintentionally revealed
by many movements. Those movements that arise
from inflamed hearts pursue in vain the goal of unity
and social justice by means of hate, injustice, and god-
lessness. Other movements pay homage (supposedly
patriotic but in reality hostile and restricted homage)
to a deity that is opposed to the Living God – a deity
that is alien to Christ and inimical to him.

Hos. 4:12

The heart needs to be transformed
The veil must fall away – the cover that darkens the
heart and restricts it to itself or to groups bound
together by blood ties or a common lot. Nothing
must hinder the outlook toward God. God the Father
of Jesus Christ can be seen only by looking with a

Eph. 4:18
2 Cor. 3:14–18

resolute and unfaltering heart toward the perfect unity of his kingdom, a unity free from all arbitrary boundaries, having as its one goal an all-embracing justice – the result of the divine joy of perfect love to friend and foe. This free outlook presupposes and demands a complete liberation of the heart from every false emotional tie, yes, a complete change of heart by means of the new birth that takes place through the Holy Spirit. The heart must not be allowed to remain as it is. It must experience the healing transformation that frees it from all impure growth and all egotistical isolation of one or more persons – even of many people or groups of people – who set their own limits at will. The heart must be "circumcised," purified, and consecrated if it wants to be truly free. It must be freed from all the rank growth of self-will and self-glorification.

Jer. 29:13–14

Luke 6:27–31

John 3:5

Titus 3:5

Rom 2:29

The Odes of Solomon, an early Christian song collection of the second century, witnesses in a profound way to this circumcision of the heart:

> My heart was circumcised and its flower appeared.
> Grace sprang up in it
> And brought forth fruit for the Lord.
> For the Most High cut me by his Holy Spirit
> And opened my reins toward him.
> He filled me in his love
> And his circumcision became my salvation.
> I hastened on the way of his peace,
> On the way of truth.
> From beginning to end
> I received his knowledge.
> I was firmly established on the rock of truth,
> Where he himself set me up.

The Lord renewed me with his raiment
And created me by his light.

From above he refreshed me with immortality
So I became like a land
That blossoms and rejoices in its fruit.
Like the sun upon the face of the earth,
The Lord gave light to mine eyes,
And my face received the dew;
My breath delighted in the precious odors of the Lord.

He led me into his paradise,
Where the pleasure of the Lord abounds.
I threw myself before the Lord
For the sake of his glory, and I said:
"Blessed are they that are planted in thy land,
That have a place in thy paradise,
That grow like the growth of thy trees
And have stepped from darkness into light!

"Behold, all thy workers are fair
And do good works.
From unkindness they turn to the strength of thy love.

"They cast off the bitterness of the trees
When they were planted in thy land.
For there is much room in thy paradise,
And there is nothing that is useless therein,
But everything is filled with thy fruits!"[12]

Therefore Fichte said: "As long as a man wants to
be something for his own sake, his true nature and
his true life cannot develop in him, and for this very

---

12 *The Early Christians: In Their Own Words*, edited by Eberhard Arnold
(Plough, 1997), 272–273.

reason he also remains cut off from blessedness."
Fichte sees all selfishly isolated existence quite rightly
as nonexistence because it is deadly restriction and

Matt. 5:20
a cutting off from the only true existence. It is only
in blessed community with the Divine Being that

1 Pet. 2:9–10
the greatest inner freedom can exist, replacing the
unhappiness of sensual self-love and the insensitivity

Rom. 8:13, 24
of moralistic legalism. Circumscribed self-love and
heartless legalism are the enemies of the gospel of
unity and freedom. The true freedom of a heart ruled

Heb. 8:10
by God does away with superficial legalism. An inner
urge that comes from perfect love replaces it: the
impulse of the Holy Spirit that leads to the divine

Col. 3:14–15
order of a common life in complete community.
Here all isolation and all arbitrary limitations are so
thoroughly overcome through the unity of the Holy
Spirit that the church and the kingdom are proved to
be the only true existence, the only true life. For it is
God's love that reveals itself in the unity of his church

Eph. 4:1–6
and his kingdom.

This experience of God is that decisive enrichment
of the inner life without which even the most gifted
heart must starve inwardly. The inner acceptance of
the Living One means rebirth for a dead heart, so that

Ezek. 11:19
it becomes a new, different heart. It cannot be a good
and upright heart until it has experienced a complete
turnabout, a wholehearted conversion that leads it
away from false narrowness within its own self to

Joel 2:12–13
true breadth, to the experience of God, who is greater

1 John 3:19–20
than our hearts. The heart needs to be redeemed
from its stubborn self-life because only in community
with the perfect life can it be restored to health. The
perfect life is love. The omnipotent breadth and

depth of God's greatness is revealed as love. In Christ and his Spirit, a complete uniting (as the church and the kingdom) is brought so near to us by love that together we are able to go this way of love.

1 John 4:16

On the path of faith, the heart is led away from the inner resistance it puts up against perfect love, and closer and closer to openhearted, voluntary obedience. The obedience that springs from faith opens up to the heart of God and to the heart of his kingdom. It is only through experiencing the free gift of God's love that the human heart can be purified of its stubbornness and despair. Only unfeigned love from the purest spheres can oust those hostile elements that are the opposite of love: self-will, which is wrapped up in itself, and impure passion of all kinds, which destroys, root and branch, its own life-energy as well as that of its victims.

Rom. 6:16–18

Ps. 42:5

Grace gives strength unto death

The gift that comes from the purifying and liberating love of the Most High is grace. In this one short word, the Bible encompasses the wealth of God's heart, which wants to give itself to us in love. It is in grace that God draws near to us. The hardship of our times and the abundance of tasks it brings show us how forlorn we are in the world, and how helpless, without God. In judgment, grace becomes the deepest need of our hearts. It is only through the free, communal gift of the Holy Spirit to his church that the hardship of our times becomes an invigorating mineral bath, immersing us in the salty strength of the future kingdom of God so that in complete community we can carry out here and now the tasks

Rom. 3:24:14–15

2 Cor. 8:9

James 2:13

of justice. The greater the need and distress become, the nearer draws the kingdom of God. The nature of grace is disclosed in the bitter fate of one who was

Heb. 2:9 crucified, in the way he sacrificed himself completely to the greatest of all tasks. When the heart experiences the freeing power of his death, scripture calls

Heb. 10:19–23 it being sprinkled with the blood of the Redeemer. Taking firm hold of unity with Christ through his death, the heart puts the whole of life into militant action against those powers that put Jesus to death. Consequently, this baptism of blood means not only being ready to die for him, but something even more immediate – being prepared time and again to

Heb. 12:3–4 risk life itself in the fight against those powers that

Matt. 20:22 oppose the kingdom of God. For us there is no other basis for true peace of heart than this fight to the bitter end. Right to the point of death by martyrdom, the strength for this fight is gained from unity with Christ in his death, from the direct nearness of God's

Phil. 3:10 heart. Only the cross brings perfect trust in God. Here, in the sharpest judgment of his wrath over all that is evil, God reveals loving grace to all people as his innermost nature.

God himself lives through his Spirit in a heart that is united in this way with the cross. His love is poured

Rom. 5:5 out in it. In the midst of murderous opponents of peace and justice, a heart filled like this remains

Acts 7:60 joyful in love, in a love that includes all enemies. To this joy and this love the martyrs of both early Christianity and the Radical Reformation have testified a thousandfold. This fundamental strengthening of character, proven at that time in death, lets the heart unfold all its powers-to-be with the zeal of inner fire

in order that, in life as in death, they may make an Rom. 14:8
impact on the whole world. The reason Christ died
for all was so that those who live may no longer live
for themselves but for him who died and rose again
for their sakes. That the whole of life up to the very 2 Cor. 5:15
brink of death is meant here, life with all its capabili-
ties and activities, is shown by the other word of
the same apostle of Jesus Christ. According to this
word, the same people who have just previously let
themselves be used in the service of unrighteousness
from now on give themselves to God in the service of
righteousness. For this is the only way the work of the Rom. 6:13, 19
Holy Spirit can and will be continually built up anew
as it once was in Jerusalem, no matter how often
Jerusalem is destroyed and no matter how often his
church is driven apart by violence.

This wealth of power and effective action up to the
very threshold of death cannot be won unless, as in
the primitive church, complete inner concentration
and perfect accord prevail in the heart. We know Acts 2–4
from the history of war that the strongest political
power is nothing but a helpless mass of people if a
united will is lacking or has been lost. Such was the
case in the World War. Such was the experience of
cities and countries in times of siege. And so, too, the
Protestant princes and cities were once "wonderfully
favored by circumstances" for the Smalkaldic War:
never, since the time of the emperors of Hohen-
staufen and the Salian emporers, had the tribes of
North and South Germany united in such a compact
mass against the crown. At that time, too, a war
council torn by conflicting interests was to blame for
the inevitable catastrophe of defeat.

A decisive heart

Consequently, only when the heart ceases to let opposing interests split it apart can even the richest powers and gifts be a help and blessing to it. If the heart wants to win the victories of a faith that has courage unto death, it needs the wholehearted decisiveness of a unified will. We cannot serve two masters at once. We cannot pursue two ideals. We cannot seek two goals in two directions. The kingdom of God, as the final kingdom, does not tolerate in any heart any other kingdom besides itself. The way of Jesus is the only way that knows no byways, no wrong ways, and no devious ways. However many roads may lead to Rome or anywhere else – there is only *one* kingdom, there is only *one* way: the complete uniting of all believers in all the activity that goes on in the heart and in life as a whole. Through the decisive outpouring of the Holy Spirit, all believers became so much *one* heart and *one* soul that they proved the uniting of all their powers, not only in the word of the apostles and in prayer, but also in the breaking of bread and in community – in full community of goods too.

Only when there is an integrated will that is decided for God and united with all similar wills can the heart profess to seek God and his kingdom. He will reveal himself powerfully only through those who have turned an undivided heart toward him. An undivided heart does not tolerate a divided life. Only those who surrender to God as their king with all their thoughts and feelings, all their powers, gifts, and goods in order to live truly for *God*, as integrated characters with an integrated life, are truly with him.

Matt. 6:24

John 14:6

John 18:36

John 7:17

Rom. 10:10

Deut. 6:5–9

The whole heart has to be converted before it is possible to follow him. Where the whole heart is turned toward him, it means that a life that is undivided (with all the powers of the spirit and all the wealth and capacities of soul and body) devotes every area of its existence to his rulership and to the church. That includes professional and vocational activity with all the skills involved in it; it includes our worldly belongings and all our temporal possessions.

Unless we stand firmly with God, we cannot carry out our service to him; it is possible to do his will in everything only when we love him heart and soul. No one can do this in his or her own strength. If we are going to give all our strength and goods, we need strength from the Holy Spirit. This strength does not proceed from us but is given to us in the word of the apostles and in the community of prayer and the breaking of bread. Whoever knows what it is to pray from a simple, undivided heart becomes grateful to God for his works and words and finds his happiness in worshiping the greatness of God and doing his will. Nothing will be impossible to one who prays this kind of prayer, the prayer that listens to God with heart and soul. Such prayer gives the inner life the boundless wealth of the truth of God. It leads the heart to the knowledge that truth is unshakable because it is the very essence of life. It has the power to accomplish everything. The impossible becomes possible. Unity is given a place in a torn world. Community in the fullest sense is created and built up, causing the unity of God's Spirit to shine out in our work and production as the reality of the church, as the city on the hill.

1 Sam. 7:3

Mark 12:28–34, 43–44

1 John 3:21–22

Eph. 3:20–21

Mark 11:22–24

John 17:21

Matt. 5:14–15

If we want to wage the spiritual wars of Jehovah and to win the land for him, we must acclaim him with our whole heart! When his will rules in our heart, he will give our inner being a wealth of experience and action that it can attain only under God's

Eph. 3:16–17 rulership. It is only when our heart is filled with and ruled by Jesus Christ as our Master that we can be equipped and qualified for the great tasks that will inevitably confront us in the difficulties of these

Rev. 22:17 times and the hardships of the future. What these tasks comprise is nothing less than the call to the

Matt. 6:33 kingdom of God and the task of his church.

Soul and Spirit

Life will prevail over death
The question of life and death is bound to concern us more than ever before: war has brought death to so many who were in the prime of life; hunger, unemployment, and shame have led to increased suicide; men and women have been killed in street battles and political conflicts; and crime against life has increased atrociously, as has crime against the life of unborn children. While the question of life and soul is one that people have wrestled with throughout the ages, the seriousness of the present time should make everything else drop into the background so that we can concentrate fully on what soul, spirit, and life mean to us.

Is it not one of the most astonishing facts that death should overcome life? Children cannot understand death. Least of all can they see how it is possible to kill people in the service of a higher cause. But even apart from this, to children the thought that human life can one day come to an end is always unreal and contrary to the truth. The unnaturalness of dying is too remote from the simplicity of their affirmation of life. For the same reason, the heathen of old with their zest for life believed in the immortality of the soul. Likewise Goethe, who was very much akin to them, declared his life conviction to Eckermann: "I agree with Lorenzo de Medici that all those who have no hope for a life beyond are dead to this life as well."[1] Life itself witnesses to its own invincible power. Hope is the hallmark of all living things.

As long as we want to deny that life is eternal, everything that belongs to life remains cloaked in tormenting riddles. Eternity remains the deepest longing of the human spirit. When we know that we are immortal beings, everything we experience is great and understandable; when we see ourselves as mortal, it all becomes dark and futile. If there is no other future and no other world (which is bound to be victorious because it is the better world), then the injustice that prevails makes nonsense of human existence by giving final victory to "the worst of all possible worlds."[2]

In the inner and outer circumstances of life, every living person can learn to recognize this other world. Fichte has declared that we only need to rise to the consciousness of a pure, moral character to find out who we ourselves are and to find out that this globe with all its glories, that this sun and the thousands of thousands of suns that surround it, that this whole immense universe, at the mere thought of which our sentient soul quakes and trembles – that all this is

Margin references: 1 John 1:2 · Wisd. of Sol. 9:14–18 · Rom. 1:18–20

---

1 Johann Peter Eckermann, 1792–1854, *Conversations with Goethe.*

2 Arthur Schopenhauer, 1788–1860, *The World as Will and Idea*, vol. 2, chapter 47.

nothing but a dim reflection in mortal eyes of our
own *eternal* existence, which is hidden within us
and which is to be unfolded throughout all eternity.
And the other way around, this is the truth given to
humankind since primeval times: our so very small
world can be nothing else than a likeness – bungled,
it is true, but nevertheless recognizable – of a bigger,
truer, and more genuine world that is not limited
by time and space. Our small world belongs to this
bigger one and must correspond to it once again.
For all of us, there is "the moral code within us and
the starry heavens above us"[3] to bring home a living
intimation of this fact of eternity.

Our life has its roots in eternity. Its nature
presumes imperishability. In space, the human spirit
goes far beyond all comprehensible limits. And similarly, the absoluteness of the moral demands it makes
knows no limit. The most certain of all certainties
known by our spirit is this: that the ray of truth, the
power of life, and the demand of the holy "thou shalt"
come to us continually anew from a living world that
lies beyond all space and nevertheless embraces all
space. With this energy that comes from absolute
authority, the human spirit follows the stream of
time long before the beginning and far beyond the
end, going outside all boundaries. This is the spirit's
most crying need: the origin of all things before the
beginning of time and the goal of the future at the
end of time.

The thirsting soul pants for its original fountain-
head and for the estuary toward which it streams. If it
has awakened to consciousness of its true self and its

Wisd. of Sol.
2:23

1 Cor. 2:4–5

John 1:1–3
Rev. 21:6
Ps. 42:1–2

---

3 Immanuel Kant, 1724–1804, *Critique of Practical Reason.*

divine destiny, it perceives in death an enemy of life, an enemy that is unnatural and that fights against the very nature of things. And it sees the same in everything else that tries to sully and destroy the clarity and purity of the eternal. Everything in our present time and in our earthly space that opposes the soul's holy "thou must" and "thou shalt" must and shall be overcome (as the soul ultimately believes it will be) by the kingdom of God at the end of all ages and beyond all earthly things. The "heavenly kingdom" of the *other* world intervenes in temporal and earthly life as the power of the *future* world. It wants to transform life here and now according to the image of what is beyond and to come. This happens as soon as and as long as the soul lets faith rule in it, whenever and wherever that may be. This other life, which is already possible here and now, means freedom for the soul. But there will never be any such soaring of a free soul as long as an atmosphere antagonistic to life both robs it of its breath and obscures its view into the eternal and everlasting.

The freedom and power of a believing soul goes so far that it expects – with the prophetic Spirit – a holy transformation to justice and unity. It expects this also for every detail of material existence in space and time. It is in the hope of the kingdom of God that the soul discovers its life. To the soul, the end of all the ways of God is unity in a tangible and visible form. For that reason, the Bible traces the death of the body back to the fact that sin as separation – as division and isolation – has brought a fatal breach into the living cohesion of creation. To the soul, evil is a power hostile to life, one that carries with it the danger of

1 Cor. 15:26

Heb. 12:26–29

1 Tim. 4:8

Tit. 3:5–7

Rom. 8:11

Rom. 6:23
Prov. 8:35–36

Ezek. 18:4–13

eternal death by separating us from God and from
one another. Sin is crime against life and love. That
was the reason why the first son born to those human
beings who separated themselves from God inevitably
became his brother's murderer.

Gen. 4:3–16

1 John 3:14–15

Nevertheless, the ancient scriptures of truth
maintain that it is impossible to extinguish the life
that God has given us out of his own nature. From
generation to generation, physical death comes to
everyone as a consequence of separation from God.
The body does indeed die when the soul leaves it.
The body that is left behind without the soul must
fall to dust. Death can never deny that its nature is
to separate by division and disintegration, and this it
has proved since the very beginning through man's
separation from God. Yet death is not annihilation.

The writings of both the Old Testament and the
New Testament speak again and again about the
souls of the dead. Every living soul has a capacity for
future life. All vital movements of humankind look
to the future. Whenever the soul comes to new life in
the Spirit, it waits for God's future. And even if the

Rev. 6:9

Rev. 20:4

James 5:7–8

Heb. 11:13–16

soul cannot believe wholeheartedly in the coming
kingdom, faith tries to salvage this or that small frag-
ment of the world-to-come and then clings to it all
the more passionately. If people are not yet ready to
fight and die for the final kingdom of love and justice,
they cling to a communistic state of the future or a
Third Reich of national freedom and racial alliance.
And in the same way, a remnant of faith in immortality and the other world emerges again and again,
even in the most unbelieving, and this they can never
lose entirely. Something in our being is meant to

continue as an active force forever. Our divine home calls us homeward. The spirit wants to return to God, in whom it has its origin. And though God himself is not yet recognized, there is at least an attempt to represent a little of his infinite significance even when it is done by idolatry.

Today, too, we have every reason to recall the faith in eternity and infinity that characterized the early Christians. If we want truth and seek it regardless of the unfounded prejudices of our time, we must and will recognize that here among the early Christians a glimpse into ultimate reality is given. In the face of this reality, no living soul can maintain its opposition. For here the soul is face to face with the life-giving Spirit of Jesus Christ. Those who believe in Jesus will live even though they die. And the day is coming when they will awake and arise to a perfect life in an immortal body. The spirits of the just who have departed this life are at rest in the Living God and wait for the day of his future. The character of this perfect life in the kingdom of God is shown by the parable of the wedding and its joyful uniting, by the comparison with the Meal of Fellowship, and by the establishment of the thrones; it is a life ruled by a love and a justice that bring about complete unity. In this kingdom, at the end of all things, the one Holy Spirit will master and pervade everything. What constitutes life now is the soul (that is, the life) in the blood, but *then* it will be the spirit, and instead of ruling over the soul's human body, the spirit will rule over a *spiritual* body.

In the kingdom, the blowing Spirit takes the place of the coursing blood. The Spirit does away with

Eccles. 12:7

John 6:68

John 11:25–26

2 Cor. 5:4–5

1 Thess. 4:16–17

Rev. 19:6–9

Rev. 20:4

Lev. 17:11, 14

1 Cor. 15:44–57

John 6:63

fluctuating emotional ties and puts in their place
a unity kept constantly alive, a unity that is just as
active as it is perfectly clear. In such a body of unity,
those who are at all times united in their Master
and serve him under his rulership live in a radically
different way from those who, far away from God, are
going to ruin, body and soul. Because these last have
rejected the unity of life, they themselves have chosen
death and separation. But even this second death
cannot mean annihilation: even this death must show
that its nature is separation and division. No more
dreadful fate for a living soul can be imagined than to
be cast out for all eternity from the life that is in God.

To be excluded forever from the center of life is
eternal death. Hell is nothing but the continuation of
the lives of those who live for themselves. Their whole
existence consists in the worm of decomposition
and decay, the worm that does not die, the burning
and consuming fire that is not quenched, and the
judgment that means dissolution and separation.
Simply because he had kept his riches to himself, the
rich man – outside whose door the beggar Lazarus
lay – met this eternal death. Ignoring the need of
others, he had enjoyed his riches as his rightful possession. The only thing he had neglected to do was to
give up all his goods to become one with the poor.

Only the person who sells everything and gives
it to the poor can gain treasure in heaven, which is
none other than life in God. Jesus challenges every
rich young man to this absolutely necessary action.
Only in this way can he join the itinerant, property-
free community of Jesus, the unity of those who
follow him. Humanly speaking, to go this way is and

Rom. 8:2–13

Dan. 12:2

Mark 9:43–48
Isa. 66:24

Luke 16:19–31

1 Tim. 6:9–10
Matt. 19:21–26

always will be quite impossible for young or old who own something valuable. But with God all things are possible. History proves it. Wealth is death because it isolates the heart from the need and distress of others

James 5:1–5 and so isolates it from love. But God will and can give life even to the richest by calling them out of this death. He frees them from it by leading them to the love that surrenders everything in perfect trust.

The spirit God has breathed into us

How does it happen that God with his unlimited life takes hold of our limited existence and fills it? We must be perfectly clear about the answer to this question and all its consequences. God is life. Only

Acts 17:28 in him do we live, move, and have our being. Physical
Job 12:7–10 life throughout nature, like all life, has its origin
Ps. 148:2–5 and being in God alone. God does not disown his
2 Pet. 3:7–13 creation. He will lead it through fire to a new day. But the soul owes its decidedly unique life in a very special way to a direct communication from God. It
Gen. 2:7 is from God that we have the breath of life. He is the Father of spirits. Just as he created the hosts of heaven with his breath, so on earth humankind received spirit from him in the same way.

Our life is not limited to the blood that courses
Wisd. of Sol. through our veins. The blowing breath of God,
15:8–11 breathed into us as spirit, is deeper. It is this spirit that takes up our calling in life. It is the spirit's calling
James 2:26 that has to determine the life of the human soul. The blood must not be allowed to rule over this calling. It has to serve it. Otherwise it ruins it. It is not without significance that in the first pages of the Bible the word *spirit* and the word for *soul* interchange in describing God's act of creation that breathed his

breath into man. The breath we have from God is
spirit *and* soul. For this spirit that was breathed into
our soul is the soul's unique life, its deepest life.   1 Cor. 2:10–14
 It is man's spirit that controls his soul and gives it
distinction. Here is the boundary line between man
and beast. Animals, too, have blood and a soul. What
they lack is the spirit, which is more than reason and
understanding. The shedding of the blood of animals   1 Cor. 1:26–30
is a responsible business, but anyone who sees the
sacrifice of slaughtered animals as similar to killing
people and can see only a relative difference between
these two things – a difference of degree – has
betrayed the spirit that God has given to humans, and
humans alone, of all terrestrial beings. We have been
placed above the animals. Our spirit is meant to rule   Gen. 1:26
over the animals. However, we can do so only under
one condition, and we can accept the ultimate sacrifice from them – the sacrifice of their blood – only
under this one condition: that our life is given to
the tasks of the spirit and that, as God's image, we
conquer the earth for God's kingdom. But whoever
kills people lays violent hands on the countenance of
God. He commits a sacrilege against the task of the   Gen. 9:6
spirit, for the spirit wants to bring all people together
and unite them. For no person is without spirit.   Rom. 8:14–17
When we cooperate with every breath of God's Spirit,
it becomes impossible for us to fight with murderous
intent and kill each other. We are given to each
other to become united in life, because human spirit
belongs to human spirit. The Spirit of God unites one
human spirit to another by ruling over them.
 The human spirit is meant from now on to rule
as the higher power over all lower powers of the soul
and unite them under its dominion. This was known

Rom. 7:5–6

as early as in Aristotle's time. It is simply impossible for a mere product of the soul's lower faculties to be the distinguishing feature of the human soul. The spirit cannot deny its origin. Therefore to be ruled by the blood or to allow base or superficial things to satisfy us completely is unworthy of our calling. Everything that betrays and destroys community in the spirit is seen as base. Therefore we see as bestial and worse than bestial every debasement that takes place through the unbridled urges of the soul in the blood. More than any madness, it tramples our higher calling in the dust.

The human spirit separated from God

The human spirit has the very greatest of destinies: God and his kingdom. Like the satanic spirit Lucifer, however, this spirit with such a high destiny has turned away from the Highest and precisely for this reason has become a rich breeding ground for the antigod principle. Separated from God, we seek ourselves and our own kingdom. We profess what is high and noble but without the rule and unity of God. We strive for the exaltation of man without giving recognition to God's deeds. We live for human self-redemption without honoring and accepting the deed of Jesus Christ and his redemption. For the people of our own race and blood or our own class, we are ready to sacrifice human life, rejecting God's kingdom and God's people.

Isa. 14:13–15
2 Cor. 11:3

In these days of ours, it should be plain to everyone that all these ideals of the human spirit that are separated from God have come to nothing. They have come to nothing in their concept of world

peace without Christ. They have come to nothing
in their efforts toward justice and freedom without
his kingdom and his church. They have come to
nothing in their illusion of an international unity
without unity in the Spirit of Truth. Prosperity in
a people united by race is founded on property and
selfish advantage. In just the same way, the worldwide
economic unity of high finance has been built up
on the material prosperity of individuals and their
mutual advantage. Even a proletarian Internationale
composed of various elements has used its solidarity
much more for material advantage in the present, for
a fraction of the underprivileged (even if it is a large
fraction), than for the justice of the future that shall
embrace all people.

Now when in the face of all this, the policy of
isolation makes nations try to close the frontiers of
the earth in an effort to establish their economic
self-sufficiency, they deny that the earth belongs
to God. They deny that God's will is to be the God   Ps. 24:1
of all people and that the will of his kingdom is to   Isa. 45:22–23
unite all nations in mutual service and make the
products of their work the common property of all.
It is impossible, though, for humankind to become
an integrated world society, a world community of
the spirit, unless it allows God's Spirit to reprove it,   Isa. 25:7–8
judge it, and rule it. God's rule, however, means that   Ps. 7:8–9
no one seeks his own advantage anymore, that no
one seeks privileges for himself anymore, and that
self-preservation is nowhere placed above the Spirit's
cause – that of unity.   1 Cor. 10:24, 26

Right up to the present day, there is no political
element of worldwide importance that follows this

way of God's world-rulership. Consequently, every
great movement with a hope for justice has inevitably
met defeat again and again. In just the same way,
every kind of national self-redemption has come to
grief – and will repeatedly come to grief – because,
in setting up an idolatry that is supposed to bring
recovery to the world, it rejects and even spurns the
very nature of divine liberation and healing. As long
as the rulership of God and his kingdom are put in
the background, efforts toward human progress of
any kind will inevitably break down over and over

Matt. 16:25   again. All human efforts toward salvation are doomed
to fail because, in their delusion, they presume to lead
people to the heights – not with God, but with the
power of idols. Faith in the masses, faith in blood, or
faith in any other power that is without the Spirit of
God, will be annihilated in the fire of the future. All
kinds of false beliefs break down under the horrors of
war, but annihilation in the fire of the future will be
still more thorough.

Human spirits unite in God's Spirit
However, what remains indestructible in all the waves
of battle that surge around us is the spirit, which will
be the first thing in us to surrender to God's will.
Here and there in all parties, the inner depths of the
spirit are already beginning to open up. The spirit is
awakening. Its will is aroused. It is still blinded by a
confusion of spirits. It is still benighted by separation
from God. But the hour is near when the spirits of
people far and wide will be gripped and called by the

Joel 2:28–30   Spirit of God.

    The fact that the soul is tied in two directions is
the cause of all the confusion that hinders this call.

Through the spirit the soul is drawn to God on the
one side, and through the blood it is bound to what
is physical and material on the other side. In this
dilemma, it remains dangerously exposed to unspiritual movements that continually attack it and try to
sever it from the Spirit of God.   James 4:1–8
The physical and material is not the real enemy
of the soul. It is merely the area that the soul has to
bring under control as its task. Rather, the enemy of   1 Pet. 2:11
life is the corruption of soul that thwarts all efforts
to accomplish this task. It is only since the soul   Matt. 16:26
has become degenerate that it has come under the
oppressive power of the physical and material. From
the beginning, it has been an accepted fact that body
and soul pervade each other, but originally it was
the spirit that was meant to rule over body and soul.
Through repressing the spirit, the diseased soul has
brought things to such a pass that the spiritual life
nowadays is enslaved to physical conditions.   2 Pet. 2:18–19
   Our turbulent times today show much more
clearly than more settled times can how no human
spirit and no movement coming from a human spirit
can ever boast of being free and independent through
its own efforts. People today are bound to the pecu-
liarities of their race and nation; they are dependent
on their economic situation and on their privileged – or underprivileged – education for their mode
of life and physical strength; they are influenced by
powers of suggestion coming from other people or
from big national movements; not least of all, they
are at the mercy of their natural disposition and their
own psychophysical makeup; and they are bowed
down on all sides, both within and without, under
the power of forces that are hostile to the Spirit. All

2 Cor. 3:17
this is in itself proof that only God and his Spirit can
bring freedom.

Gal. 5:13
Any other freedom is a lie. The only possible
way for the individual consciousness to become
free from its servitudes and for the nations and the
masses to become free from enslavement is through
the community of human spirits with God's Spirit!
Without this direct oneness with the whole, the
individual soul remains enslaved, impoverished, and
limited, just as does the collective soul of a family
group, or a nation, or a class, or any other combination. All other combinations of people and strength
lead deeper and deeper into ruin through constant
escalation of mutual hostility. The highest and the
ultimate in true liberation and uniting will be given
to us only when the highest unity in God takes

Gal. 3:28
possession of us.

The human soul is a subordinate unit of
consciousness, which, in spite of all ungodly associa-
tion with kindred lives, remains lonely and thwarted
until it is bound to the superordinate unity of God.
Fechner catches in people's seeking a glimpse of this
highest unity of consciousness.[4] He sees it as the truly
eternal and unchangeable, as the One, always true
to himself, who wants to be at work in rich variety
and infinite diversity. Without God's Spirit we are
changeable, inconsistent, and unstable – unbalanced,
out of proportion, torn, and hostile within ourselves

Rom. 3:10–24
and among ourselves. Therefore it must be an experience of absolute unity and, at the same time, absolute
disparity that unites the consciousness of the soul
with God.

---

4 Gustav Theodor Fechner, 1801–1887, a German philosopher and physicist.

With such an experience, eternity is born in us, and we have to consecrate our life with complete dedication. For this experience becomes new every day – a continual new beginning. As often as we lay hold of life in God, these new beginnings, these deeds and actions, are stamped with the seal of eternity. Eternity penetrates time. The spirit of creation seeks out the life of the earth. Being filled with what God's eternal will decrees can never result in alienation from life. On the contrary, the spirit of life can lead only to an unfolding of powers in all the diversity of all life's relationships. In our families and in our professional lives, in our work and in our whole sphere of activity, in society and in community, the creative spirit wants to shape life into a productive unity.

Rom. 12:1–2

As Jacobi has expressed it:

The spirit that aspires to God
Must indeed lift himself from the dust.
But if on *earth* he does not truly live,
Neither will he live in *heaven*.[5]

Those who are gripped by God's Spirit turn to his creation with all the interest that comes from God's love. Their life has one goal: that God's kingdom shall come to rule over all people on earth, that his will shall be done in our world just as it is in the kingdom of heaven, that his name shall be honored in active recognition of his nature, that his holiness shall never be desecrated by any unholy action anywhere – rather, faith shall bring forth a love that makes God's nature recognizable through deeds.

Matt. 6:9–10

5 Johann Georg Jacobi, 1740–1814, "Gnome," in *J. G. Jacobi's Sämtliche Werke*, (1819), 150.

It is through being ruled more and more by God's Spirit, and in no other way, that the human spirit can get nearer to this high and final goal. Only the spirit that is ruled by God is able to see into the depths 1 Cor. 2:9–11 of revelation. Revealed truth was given to us on the basis of the prophetic word in Jesus Christ and in his apostolic church. God's Spirit wants to lead the human spirit into this truth in such a way that our Eph. 3:14–19 lives become filled and determined by it.

The spirit's battle for the soul

The word of God pierces a person until it divides soul and spirit asunder in order to let him or her recognize without a shadow of doubt the unspiritual sensuality of the unredeemed life of the soul and in order to set the spirit, which thirsts for freedom, face to face with Heb. 4:12–13 God's Spirit. If in our inmost being, the spirit (as the breath of God) does not stand out quite sharply and clearly in contrast to the soul (as the impure stream of our blood), we remain in the torpor of spiritual Rom. 8:9–14 death. Those emotional people who allow the unpurified life of their soul to rule them are unable to Wisd. of Sol. 1:4 receive the divine Spirit. There is no sharper contrast to the consistent wisdom that comes from God than James 3:13–17 the worldly wisdom of the soul, which inevitably gets entangled again and again in untruthfulness when it tries to bring some semblance of harmony to its contradictory aims.

The way the world situation developed during the war and after the war should make it clear to the blindest of the blind that the natural life of the soul is diametrically opposed to the life that comes from God. People believed that they had all the life they

needed in human evolution, in patriotic efforts, or in
the struggle of their class for justice, just as if they did
not need God. They presumed to lay claim to things
that are God's alone. They even wanted to decide over
the life and death of people and nations. They forgot
that it is the Lord who kills and makes alive. They
scorned the fact that God is life. Yet he alone is Lord   John 14:6
over life and death. Whoever honors him in Christ   Deut. 32:39
cannot kill any person or judge any soul. People lost
all feeling for the fact that life lies in God's hand – that
his decree alone has the right to determine the
destiny of the soul. They lost all fear of him who can
destroy body and soul, and stood before his judgment   Matt. 10:28
without awe. They lost all reverence for God.

 We know that if the sun were extinguished it would
mean instantaneous death for all life on our planet.
We admit that an old riverbed will not have running
water anymore once the stream has been diverted. It
is clear to everyone that even the best water becomes
a miserable slough if it has become disconnected from
its source. Yet we have tried to deaden our conscience
whenever it said that every lack of reverence wounds
our soul with a mortal wound. We have wanted to
forget that sin – violation of life – brings death to the
soul: it is the destruction of man.

 Unspiritual desires and the lies and deceit that go
with them, hostility and the lust to kill, mammon
and possessions – they all fight against life and soul.   Gal. 5:16–17
For these are the forces that constitute the power
inimical to life – that power that has separated itself
from God. The human spirit is bound up with the   John 8:44
life of the soul: it cannot be pure if the soul does not
live in God's purity, and every time the soul touches   Isa. 52:11–12

Matt. 6:24

the rottenness of impurity and allows itself to be contaminated, it is not living in God's purity. The spirit is then tainted along with the soul and therefore is incapable of redeeming it. The spirit lives in the soul. Everything that goes on in the soul influences the spirit and all the movements of the spirit.

Isa. 38:15–16

We should not imagine that the spiritual life can work independently of the world of body and soul as if it were in splendid isolation on an island, untouched by all that the soul experiences on the mainland. It is the entire atmosphere coming from the whole of a person that influences his or her thinking. No vibration of the soul leaves our spirit unaffected. During the second half of the nineteenth century, the brain was thought to rule from an autocratic throne over the life of the spirit. Recent research has dethroned it. The brain does not determine the soul's character or our attitude as a whole with all our most important impressions, feelings, and emotions. A sick soul can have a brain that is completely intact. The soul can be healthy even when the brain is diseased.

Ps. 13:2

2 Cor. 5:3

The Old Testament is right in saying that the heart, the blood circulation with all the special organs belonging to it, and especially the different strains in the blood itself determine the character of the soul – the spiritual personality of a person. Blood and heart can disperse melancholy of soul and depression of spirit and provide the necessary constitution and frame of mind for the highest literary achievements and even for abstract intellectual ones. Granted, the brain is a very important organ for the intellectual work of comprehending, thinking, and remembering, yet it is simply one of the tools in the life of the soul and the spirit. It is only one of its workshops or

Deut. 30:14–20

Prov. 15:13

transmitting stations, which in a special way reflects
the life of the soul and the life of the spirit; it is their
place of action.   Job 32:8
   We must not confuse the spirit with brainwork
in general or with its more specialized intellectual
functions. The human spirit represents much more
the "practical reason" of the holy "thou shalt," which,
according to Immanuel Kant, makes its incontest-
able demands with the firmness of "thou canst
because thou shalt." The spirit is not to be found in
any specific place in the body. The bearer of one's
entire soul is one's whole body. The human spirit
and the basic character of the spiritual attitude are
breathed into the entire soul as its profoundest and
most divine element. This spirit is able to prove itself   Ps. 19:7–9
extremely independent of the body, and superior to it,
as soon as it has experienced a decisive liberation.

The soul is the life of the body
Such a liberation remains an impossibility, however,
unless it embraces all areas of the soul. The human
spirit is inevitably affected by any lack of freedom
and any defilement of one's life. The soul embraces   Wisd. of Sol.
all manifestations of life. It is the bearer of everything   9:13–15
that is alive in us. The soul is the total consciousness
of the individual: the combination of all our sensual
perceptions as well as the concentration of all our
higher and spiritual relationships. There can be no
other life for the soul than in this consciousness with
all it encompasses. In this consciousness, all we experience with our feelings, thoughts, and will becomes
reality and knowledge.
   The consciousness is that undefined place where
all of a person's functions and organs are to become a

1 Cor. 12:4–26 united whole. Unity of consciousness is the secret of organic life. Unity of spirit is the secret of our calling. In a person as a living whole, we can recognize the body by the finger of the body pointing outward, the soul by the finger of the soul pointing inward, but the spirit we recognize by the finger of God pointing to Luke 11:20 his kingdom.

The life in the physical frame – that which makes it into a living body – is its soul. In countless instances therefore, the translators of the old scriptures interpreted the word "soul" as "life." The soul, being life, encompasses our spiritual existence just as much as our physical existence from birth to death. Whenever it is a question of preserving or risking life, of danger to life or loss of life, the word "soul" is used where we Mark 8:36–37 would expect the word "life."[6] That the soul is the life Lev. 17:11, 14 of an organism is testified by this scripture: "The life Deut. 12:23 of the flesh is in the blood." Just as our physical frame Gen. 9:4 without blood has no life, the body without the soul is dead.

It is not by chance that the thought of blood that is shed is more horrifying to us than the thought of the graves of the slain. We could see this in our reaction to the news of the reddening of the Masurian Lakes in the World War. In spite of an obvious scientific explanation, the reddening of the so-called Lake of Blood and War in Siberia (which is said to grow a deeper red with every great bloodshed) also makes a deep impression on people's minds. This is simply because blood and soul – the red of this special sap and the tremendous fact of life – cannot be separated. It signifies more to us to see life ebb away in a stream of blood than to stand in front of a corpse.

---

6 The author is referring to the traditional German translation of the Bible by Martin Luther (1545).

The physical body that has lost its blood has given up its soul. Mephistopheles makes Faust sell his life with a drop of blood because blood is streaming and flowing life. The evil spirit wants to have the whole of man. He wants his life. He wants his soul. For this reason he has to get hold of his blood. "Blood is a sap of quite peculiar kind."[7] Therefore, according to an old version of *Faust*, just as Faust is about to use his blood-filled quill to sign the contract with the devil, the blood congeals on his scratched hand to give a warning. It congeals in the form of the words "Flee, O man!" This cry to take flight is forced from the blood by the imminent danger of being gripped by evil. The divine life has an energy that demands more than the blood in its weakness does. The spirit demands that the soul resist to the utmost: "to resist to the point of shedding your blood in the struggle against sin."

1 Pet. 5:8–9

Heb. 12:4

Resistance unto death is exceedingly rare because the blood is bound up through the soul not only with the higher, spiritual life but just as closely or even more closely with confused feelings and the basest impulses. There is something in the blood that weakens. Those emotional people in whom the blood is not ruled by the spirit are easily led in their sympathies, becoming weak and unobjective. Because of their lack of strength for vigorous action and their limp, unmanly compliancy, they are easily led astray. The more lost a man is on the false path he has begun to tread, the more does each successive emotional weakness cause his soul to wither away.

Rom. 7:15, 18–25

Gal. 5:18–25

An enfeebled soul is swept along whenever the individual or the nation is roused inwardly by an appeal to the blood or by an insistence on blood ties.

7 Johann Wolfgang von Goethe, 1749–1832. *Faust*, Part I, line 1740.

That is why mass suggestion is so successful. Whether
it excites sexual life into degenerate licentiousness,
incites the masses to war or civil war, or shatters business habits of trustworthiness and entices people to
luxury and extravagant living – whatever it does, the
surprising result is explained by the weakness of the
emotionally unstable masses. Each time such weakness of life stirs the blood, it reveals the tyrannization
of the emotional life over the nobler element of the
spirit – in actual fact, therefore, it reveals the ignoble
servitude of our highest possession to our lower
nature.

Matt. 27:21–25

Body and soul must be ruled by the spirit

An effective renewal of life can come about only
when soul and blood are gripped and penetrated by
the highest life, coming from the spirit. This new life
must come from the spirit because only in the spirit
can freedom and clarity begin. It has to penetrate
into the blood-life of the soul if it is to be a reality in
life. For blood builds up the human body. Without
the soul or life in the blood there is no organic
connection between the spiritual life and the physical
existence of the body.

Rom. 8:11

For this reason, according to ancient mysticism,
everything that has gained power over my blood has
gained power over *me*. Here is the link between the
inner world and the outer world. If we want to master
things we have to pluck up courage and take heart:
"Blood is the sap above all saps. It can nourish daunt-
less courage in the heart."[8] The soul reveals the fact
that the blood is the natural element of all our urges

---

8 From an old version of *Faust* produced in 1690, quoted in *Goethe's
Sämtliche Werke*, vol.14, (1902), 295.

and feelings, including – not least among them – the sensual ones. Because the blood communicates with every power center of the body, a state of excitement in the blood is often an indication of an unspiritual life guided by natural instincts and impulses. The bloodstream is the nitric acid that tests whether the spirit or the body has the rulership. Whichever of the two comes through this test has won the battle.

Gal. 6:8

However precious our blood is to us and however sacred our blood ties must be, we need a life that is not guided by our senses and our blood but determined by the spirit. The life of the blood can be as thoroughly decadent as it can be noble. It bears within it the seeds of corruption. Everyone who builds on the blood is building on shifting sand. Blood is unstable and perishable. Only the spirit remains alive. The storm of the spirit is stronger than any other wind. The life of the spirit alone stands firm when all other life is doomed to destruction.

Eph. 2:3–6

1 Cor. 15:50

A different homeland

In these critical times we need more than ever a testimony to the truth that God has given an eternal life – one that cannot ebb away with the blood because it is God's life and therefore independent of the blood and the senses. According to the true testimony of the Spirit, this life is in God's Son. It comes to us through the Holy Spirit. It gives our spirit testimony of another homeland, different from the land of our blood. It makes us so truly sons and daughters of God that we can represent no other interests save those of his heart and his kingdom. The Spirit leads us to a people quite different from the

John 6:27, 40

Rom. 8:16–17

1 Pet. 2:9–10

Matt. 10:29

Rev. 6:9

Matt. 27:15–26

Matt. 24:9
John 16:2–3

people of our blood. God's eternal life unites us with the people of God whose bond is not one of blood but of the Holy Spirit. Only those who are prepared to risk life and blood can find this kingdom of the Spirit. The path this people treads is strewn with the dead, for others can and will not tolerate it that the spirit of this people conquers the land. By what he does to God's people, the god of this world has to reveal himself as the murderer from the beginning. The Spirit of Jesus Christ has never allowed his church to kill even one single person. His people, however, have continually been murdered just as Jesus himself was brought to execution by the best state (from the military and judicial point of view) and by the most outstanding nation (from a religious and institutional point of view), yes, even by the majority vote of those of his own blood.

Today also, people and nations, the state, and the institutional church will not tolerate witnesses to divine truth. It is not only the state in the East that cries out, "Away with him!" Voltaire's "*Écrasez l'infâme*" is the cry of the West. Whoever wants to represent the witness of Jesus in word and deed must be ready for death anywhere. The reason is clear: witnessing to the truth tears down all the disguises that are meant to conceal the workings of the prevailing powers.

Jesus has brought us a revelation that destroys all delusions. It exposes the true state of the world and its kingdoms, its principalities, its god and spirit, as well as the true state of every single human being. It is only under Jesus' influence that we become free of the false idea that life consists in politics and economics, in power and property, in violence and the struggle for existence, in eating and drinking, in clothing and housing, in pleasure and variety, in honor and reputation. The body is more than clothing. The soul is life and therefore more than food. The kingdom of God is more than all the kingdoms of this world. The spirit is more than the soul. What does it profit a man to gain the whole world if he forfeits his life?

Matt. 6:25–34

Matt. 16:26

Life during the World War and its aftermath of escalating need and distress freed many from a narrow-minded, bourgeois misconception: that the creature comforts of a pampered mode of life (quicker transport and communication and a good income) are necessities of life. Moreover, many consciences have been awakened from their torpid sleep and kept awake as if by a constant thunderstorm, realizing that in the face of the increasing distress everywhere they have no right to hold on to a privileged way of life. People have to come out of their castles and open the doors of their villas in order to search out and bring in those who have become destitute in the storm, those who are without work or home. A true life of community with God encompasses the inmost fortification of our stronghold as well as the outer fortifications. When our soul has been awakened to the kingdom of God, the Spirit who rules from that kingdom will have to tackle our existence and shape it according to his will down to the outermost details. His will is toward brotherly love. This transformation will be so thorough and complete that very few people can imagine it.

James 2:14–17

1 John 3:10–18

However, before we can think of a new form for our outward existence, body and soul must be taken possession of by God and changed to accord with his image. We have experienced in the history of our times how impossible it is to reconstruct an outer existence and build it up when inner strength has gone into a decline. It is not only in the Russia and in the Austria of pre-World War times that we can see how little even such great empires signify when their inner character begins to break up. What is a kingdom that is divided in itself? "What does it profit a man to gain the whole world and yet suffer harm to his soul?"

Nothing is more necessary than an inmost renewal of life. In this renewal our destiny, independent of all alien influences, shall unfold like a seed growing into a strong, firm tree, allowing our soul and its whole sphere of activity to become that which is intended. It is not in ourselves that we find the strength, inner peace, and freedom for the growth of this true and genuine life. Still less do these prevail in the world around us. Only the Living One can give them to us. Only he brings life, its fulfillment, and with it the active inner peace of his works. Only when he has become the loving, caring overseer of our soul can it find the strength it needs for a new, free, and active life. Only he leads to a life in which the soul, freed from turning around itself and circling around false planets, can live and work from the center of life.

The sacred flame
This life is God and his rulership. The light of the life given in Christ shines more brightly on our weak, selfish existence than the sun into our night. And

Rom. 12:1–2

Matt. 12:25–26

Mark 8:36

Col. 3:9–10

Eph. 4:22–24

just as the sun gives life and nourishment to this
planet, Jesus alone gives us, his brothers and sisters,
the strength and nourishment to begin a real life and
build that up in place of our previous sham existence. Eph. 4:15–16
Jesus is the bread of life for which we hunger. He John 6:35
has the water of life for which we thirst. His life, Rev. 22:17
which far exceeds all other possible ways of living,
merits our dismissing once and for all our own weak,
selfish life and all ideals restricted and determined
by our blood. We must turn away from all the will-
o'-the-wisps that flit around churchyards. We must
hold his burning light firmly in the hands of our
heart because he wants to bring life into every grave.
Nothing should be in our hands but his radiant life
because this is victorious over all the worlds of death. 1 Thess. 5:5

There is a legend about a soldier who for a long
time seemed to seek nothing but murderous battle
and vainglory. He devoted himself wholeheartedly
to war, and even when he joined a crusade, vainglory
seemed to be all he looked for. It so happened that he
was the first to scale the walls of Jerusalem. He had
the privilege of being the first to light his candle at
the altar of the Holy Sepulcher.

This flame transformed his life, though. He
forsook the princedom that beckoned him. He took
the candle. It became everything to him. He rode and
traveled roundabout ways to bring this flame to his
people without letting it go out. He was looked upon
by many as a madman as he held the burning light in
his hands wherever he went, never taking his eyes off
it. In the depths of loneliness, fallen upon by thieves,
in want and exposed to storms, in hunger and priva-
tion and mocked at by the crowds, he concentrated
on one thing: he shielded the flame. From then on he

could never have another thought but to protect every tiniest flame of holy life. His life became a light of love in vigorously working for others.[9]

John 8:12 Whoever wants to protect this flame of God's love in the soul and guard the light of life will have to show this same attitude. Once we have kindled our life from the flame of the Crucified One, his Spirit with all its powers expresses itself in an undreamed-of way that we could never learn elsewhere. It is the torch of the Spirit that shows the way then. If we want to reach the goal of our destiny we can only do it by letting his divine love unfold from within to without.

John 16:13

1 John 2:5–6

Wherever this fire is kept burning in people's hearts, it means life for the whole world. It becomes a light on a candlestick set up for everyone. It is only a uniting in complete community of faith that will bring light to the whole world as the city on the hill. Its innermost life gathers all members around the carefully protected central flame as around a campfire. Only he who protects this grail of the church knows what wealth of life God sends out into all lands from his city.

Matt. 5:14–15

God's Spirit wants to dwell within us

Once we have come to recognize God as the only element of all true life, all inner powers of the soul seek to unfold in order to come fully and completely into action, concentrated on him. The soul that is filled with God embraces the whole of life with all its activities, inner and outer, intellectual and physical. In order to bring life completely under the authority of God's vital power, its inner aspect must be brought

Ps. 16:9–11

Eph. 3:16–19

---

9 Selma Lagerlöf, 1858–1940, "The Sacred Flame."

under his influence first of all. The power of infinite
life sinks its roots into the inmost depths of the
soul before it has a strong and active influence on
external life. The confession "Thou givest my soul
great strength" can be made truthfully only when this   Ps. 138:3
strength has begun to reign in our inner being.

The inmost heart of the believing church, in
which God dwells, is like a well-watered garden, full
of quiet, peace, and security. Enemies cannot find   Isa. 58:11
the way in. A living wall of tall trees rooted in fertile
ground protects it from the storms raging outside.   Ps. 46:4–7
The noise of the world outside does not penetrate
into the secluded center of this garden, in which
God's heart has its dwelling. And yet the gates of the
garden stay wide open so that all that is living can go
in. They stay open because all the powers and capa-   Rev. 21:25–27
bilities of the soul are sent out to share in all people's
distress and bring them help wherever possible.   Isa. 61:1–2

When we speak of the life of the soul, we usually
think only of the innermost part of a believing spirit.
But we have to remember that the soul embraces the
whole of life. Then we shall understand why profound
thinkers of all times have spoken about the inmost
recesses and depths of the *soul*, about the bottom of
the *soul* and the center of the *soul* rather than about
any other seat of life.[10] The apostles of Jesus Christ
exhort the believers to become new in mind and
spirit. What the believers have to do is to search their   Eph. 4:22–24
innermost being because their life in Christ shall
be hidden in God, so that from the bottom of their   Col. 3:3
hearts they can say, "I live, yet now it is no longer I
but Christ who lives in me." The spirit is our inmost   Gal. 2:20

---

10 Where German idiomatic usage has *Seele*, or soul, English more often
   has the heart as the center of life.

treasure. When it is illuminated by God's Holy Spirit,
our spirit, and only our spirit, knows what is in us.
When it is led by the Spirit of Jesus Christ, the spirit
and only the spirit can become the lamp of God that
searches all the innermost parts of the body.

1 Cor. 2:10–12

Prov. 20:27

By and large, the heart embraces the inner aspect
of a person. Therefore we find the manifestations
of life in the heart – the thinking, feeling, and
willing, the disposition and the character of the
heart – ascribed to the soul as well. For the soul,
as the life of a person, by its very nature includes
the heart as the inner core of life. We can imagine
human life as concentric circles of different colors
superimposed on each other and enclosing each
other. Our external, material body, part of nature as
a whole, forms a comprehensive gray circle. A blue
circle denoting the organic life we have in common
with plants is just as big. The third circle, a red one,
has the same dimensions and stands for the life of
the soul in the blood, which, as a human person,
embraces the whole consciousness. This last circle of
life is characteristic of the animal kingdom as well.

With the smaller circles it is different. In contrast
to the large perimeter three times covered, the
heart forms a smaller concentric circle, perhaps best
indicated by fiery coloring. This confines itself to the
life of inner feelings and thoughts and activity of the
will, that is, the deeper part of our character. This
alone is enough to distinguish humans from all other
living creatures. The human spirit, however, forms
the center that dominates the whole. It is a secluded,
inner circle, which in view of our destiny should be
colored white. This spirit is given solely to humankind. Schiller refers to this when he says: "Once I have

searched the core of man, I know what he wants and
what he is doing." It is this core that is all-important.
God's Spirit wants to make his dwelling among us,   Ps. 51:12, 17
beginning in our spirits.   Isa. 57:15

The right relationship of soul and spirit

The higher will of the soul is spirit. The spirit is
the active and creative genius. The spirit is reason   Ps. 77:6
working constructively to meet the demands made
by religion, ethics, and society. It is the spirit that
directly perceives and experiences what is divine in
the human heart. The soul, on the other hand, gets
its feeling for life more through what is physical
and determined by the blood. It includes all our
desires and longings and also that in us which is
purely receptive. The whole reception of all the outer
stimulations of life takes place in the soul. It remains
more sensual, more closely related to the body, more
strongly rooted in the body, and more firmly bound
to it than the spirit. The spirit lives in the activity of
the highest and freest relationships and aims of the
will. It dwells in the most royal of all the chambers of   1 Pet. 3:4
the consciousness. For the spirit, the highest destiny
is to be infused with divine Spirit, to be united with
the Holy Spirit.

The consciousness of the soul is a living mirror of
all the relationships into which human life is woven.
The influence of these relationships varies greatly
according to their intensity. It is in the life of the soul
that the decision is made as to which feelings, desires,
ideals, and thoughts we allow to cross the threshold
of our innermost being.   Prov. 25:28

As long as the feelings of the soul in the blood
(which work in darkness) are controlled by the power

of the spirit ruling in our hearts, they cannot grow
into base intentions or evil deeds. Yet we see in all the
excitement of our times how these feelings wait for

Gal. 6:1
Matt. 26:41

a moment when the image of God and his influence
grow weaker in us. From that moment on, the lusts
and false ideals of the blood (allied to other powers of
darkness) can cross the threshold of our heart. They
become the will to do evil, and then they unite in evil

Ps. 78:8

action. Sin has come. "Lust when it has conceived
gives birth to sin; and sin when it is full-grown brings

James 1:15

forth death."

Joyless lust for murder and hate, poisonous
readiness to accuse one's opponents and use lies
to disparage them, loveless joy in property and all
personal privileges, impure and unspiritual lusts of
the body – all these lie in wait for the will with insa-
tiable greed. They have to capture the will with the
dazzling temptations offered by stolen and pseudo-
spiritual virtues before they can work their evil.

The soul is able to ward off these temptations
only when the will's strength to resist has found a
firm foothold in the spirit. The will can reject all

1 Pet. 4:2

the enticements of seductive mental images; it can
overcome all the temptations of murky ideals and
aims; but it can do this only when – through being
constantly reminded by the Holy Spirit – the soul's
consciousness is firmly and clearly ruled by the unity
that comes from the heart of God, by the unity of
all the thoughts of his love, by the unity of all the
pictures of his future kingdom and its powers, and

Phil. 2:1–4

by the image of Jesus with all his words and deeds.
"Strength of character depends on this, that a definite
unity of images and ideas continually occupies the

conscious mind, weakening any opposing images and
not allowing them to enter."[11] If the seductive powers
of other aspirations are not to gain admittance and
rule over our will, then the innermost chamber of
our soul must always be filled with the Spirit of Jesus
Christ. The chamber where our spirit is enthroned   Heb. 6:19
must always be filled with all his thoughts and with
his will, that is, with every impulse of his heart.   John 14:6

In such agitated times as ours today, the enemy
of our soul has a powerful band of accomplices that
wants to shatter and destroy it. But in the hush of
night God speaks clearly and unmistakably to our
soul to draw it away from destruction and make it his   Isa. 55:3
follower. He awakens the spirit and shows us the way   Prov. 7:2
to life. He wants to fill the awakened soul with his   Luke 10:25–28
peace so that dark powers have no room. When the   Rom. 8:6
soul cries out for God, driven to do so by the distress   Ps. 62:1
of our time, it will be led to the goal – to the church   Ps. 116:4
and to the kingdom – if by the will it is lifted up to
Jesus Christ and remains concentrated on him alone.   Ps. 143:8–10

---

11 A summary of the thought of the philosopher and psychologist Johann
  Friderich Herbart, 1776–1841.

Other Titles by Eberhard Arnold

God's Revolution
Justice, Community, and the Coming Kingdom
Excerpts from talks and writings on the church,
family, government, world suffering, and more.

The Early Christians
In Their Own Words
This collection of Early Christian writings challenges
readers to live more fully and radically.

Why We Live in Community
with two interpretive talks by Thomas Merton
A time-honored manifesto on the meaning and
purpose of community.

Salt and Light
Living the Sermon on the Mount
Thoughts on the "hard teachings" of Jesus
and their applicability today.

The Prayer God Answers
Rediscover the kind of prayer that has the power
to transform our lives and our world.

Plough Publishing House
PO BOX 398, Walden, NY 12586, USA
Robertsbridge, East Sussex TN32 5DR, UK
4188 Gwydir Highway, Elsmore, NSW 2360, Australia
845-572-3455 • info@plough.com • *www.plough.com*